新航道雅思考试(IELT

IELTS

雅思考试

口语练习

胡敏 主编
Nick Stirk 编著

中国广播电视出版社

图书在版编目(CIP)数据

雅思考试（IELTS）口语练习 / （英）斯特赖克（Stirk, N.）编著. —北京：中国广播电视出版社 2004.8
(新航道雅思考试（IELTS）培训系列教材 / 胡敏主编)
ISBN 7-5043-4320-X

Ⅰ. 雅… Ⅱ. 斯… Ⅲ. 英语 - 口语 - 高等学校 - 入学考试，国外 - 自学参考资料 Ⅳ. H319.9

中国版本图书馆 CIP 数据核字（2004）第 082453 号

雅思考试（IELTS）口语练习

主　　编	胡　敏
编　　著	Nick Stirk
责任编辑	樊丽萍
监　　印	尤　冲
出版发行	中国广播电视出版社
电　　话	86093580　86093583
社　　址	北京复外大街 2 号　　邮政编码：100866
经　　销	各地新华书店和外文书店
印　　刷	三河市东方印刷厂
开　　本	787 × 1092 毫米 1/16
印　　张	8.5
字　　数	165（千）字
版　　次	2004 年 9 月第 1 版　2004 年 9 月第 1 次印刷
书　　号	ISBN 7-5043-4320-X / H · 171
定　　价	18.00 元

雅思风暴

（丛书序）

胡 敏

1999年留学热潮席卷国内，雅思考试悄然兴起，它的中文全称是“国际英语水平测试系统”，英文缩写为“IELTS”，专为留学与移民英联邦国家的申请者设置。这一年恰恰是我在新东方最忙碌的一年，主讲托福阅读，创办四、六级和考研英语培训项目，还要面对大量的教学与管理工作。在这种情况下，校领导多次找我，希望我能把雅思做起来，因为这项考试注重综合能力，要研发它必须有多年的学术底蕴和教学经验，他们认为我是最佳人选。

经过考虑，我接下了这个项目。当时国内雅思培训刚刚起步，第一个培训班开课时，根本没有可以信赖的教材，基本上是边上课边编教材。两个月培训结束，第一套内部教材也基本搞定，教学效果还算不错。

为了更进一步了解雅思，保证培训质量，我决定到位于英国伦敦的雅思考试主管机构——英国文化委员会走一趟。经过调研，我了解到英国文化委员会雅思总裁名叫肖恩·海德，通过国际友人的引荐，肖恩·海德接见了我。坐在他对面，我把事先准备好的问题提了出来，他一一作答，聊到托福考试时，肖恩·海德说了一句话：“TOEFL is an empire.（托福是一个帝国。）”言下之意雅思无法与之抗衡。

我则充满信心地说：“雅思考试具备巨大的市场潜力，肯定会异军突起。”

听了我的话，肖恩·海德开心地笑了。

之后我访问了剑桥大学考试委员会，走遍了几乎所有相关书店，购买了大量雅思考试类书籍。当我离开英国时，知道自己已经尽了最大努力，拿到了雅思的核心资源，可以把培训做得更好了。

归国航程9个小时，我没有休息，而是抓紧时间学习带回来的书。回国后，第1件事就是着手研发国内第1套真正意义上的雅思教材。由于客观条件及时间限制，它借鉴了国外雅思教材的部分内容，但我相信，假以时日，我肯定会研发出完全本土化的雅思教材。

教材开发完成，我开始全国巡回演讲。根据我对雅思的理解，我总结了4句话概括雅思：留学新途径、移民直通车、外企通行证、英语大课堂。演讲中我反复说明雅思考试的科学性：能够全面评估应试者的语言能力和水平，参加有些语言考试可能会高分低能，但参加雅思考试一定是高分高能。这次巡回演讲，我的足迹踏遍大江南北，先后举办了数十场免费演讲，使国人对雅思有了更多的了解，同时为英语培训开辟了一个新的领域，在国内掀起了第1场雅思风暴。

2001年，在充分准备之后，我认为研发拥有自主知识产权的雅思教材的时机已经成熟，经过我领导下的研发团队夜以继日的努力，终于完成了第2代雅思教材的编写。这套教材共17本，经测试，题目的仿真度达到85%以上，仅这一点就是许多国内外培训机构至今未能达到的。这套教材因其独创性、可操作性和高效性，很快在学员当中赢得了巨大的知名度，许多已经在国外学习的学员，也回国求购这套教材。与此同时，雅思成绩先后受到多个国家的承认，这种内外呼应的结果是，雅思考试如日中天，考生对雅思学习的热情一浪高过一浪。也就是在这个时候，学员和同行开始称呼我为“胡雅思”，这可以说是我在雅思领域制造的第2场风暴。

2002年澳大利亚宣布根据雅思成绩录取留学生，受这个消息的鼓舞，6月我亲赴澳大利亚，到各个学府与同行深入交流，广泛接触中国留学生。接触中我发现，留澳学生年龄普遍偏小，语言基础薄弱。回国后，我马上设计并建立了全国第1个雅思基础班培训基地，全面解决低龄学员的学习问题。第1期招生就爆满，2个月里招了近千名学生，在业内引起巨大轰动，许多培训机构争相模仿这种教学模式。同时我的第3代雅思教材也被隆重推入市场，由此全国各地雅思培训进入爆发期，仅新东方暑期雅思培训就达3万人，许多海外学子纷纷回国接受培训，其他雅思培训机构也出现了前所未有的井喷。

雅思风暴三度抢滩成功，一举成为培训业的宠儿。各大报刊争相刊登我在雅思培训方面的言论，一家主流媒体甚至刊登了一篇题为《雅思风暴，胡敏制造》的文章来形容当时的学习热潮。最近出版的《中国民办教育生存报告》说：“在过去的几年里，这个长着细长眼睛和高高额头的家伙旋风般地成为雅思考试的代名词。”那段时间，我每次参加网上举办的对话活动，短短一两个小时就会有成千上万的问题涌入聊天室，学员们的学习热情使我深受感动。曾经有个年轻人在学校找了我十多天，把他的雅思听力理解教材拿出来给我看，里面做满了各种记号，笔迹力透纸背，把书都划破了。而在此之前他一句英语都不懂，一个单词没学过，完全是靠毅力和信念的支撑，最大程度地信任了我所教授的方法，在3个月内使自己的雅思成绩达到了5.5分。我一辈子都不会忘记这个年轻人，从表面上看，是我总结出来的学习方法让他获益良多，在我看来，是他的积极向上、永不服输让我再一次感受到了功夫不负有心人。

时至今日，雅思考试在全国建立了25个考点，每年举办35次考试，已经有了与托福平分秋色的态势。而在英联邦留学的人员当中有70%以上参加过我主持的雅思培训，绝大部分雅思考生学习过我主编的教材。回想我制造的一场又一场雅思风暴，再看看自己接受的一次又一次洗礼，我深深体会到了弄潮人的快乐与幸福。

2004年9月于北京

Preface

This book contains the same topics and questions as in the Speaking Book in this series. A sample answer has been provided for each question. Always remember that there are many ways to answer the questions in this book and in the actual IELTS speaking module. Contrary to popular belief, there is never a 'right' answer to any of the questions.

In the IELTS speaking module, just as in the writing module, the examiner will expect you to be able to give reasons to support your opinions and develop your answers. The main reasons for developing your answers are that you want to show the examiner your vocabulary and range of grammar. Developing your answers also allows you to use connectives to show cohesion.

The answers contain useful vocabulary which you can and should use in your own answers. Do not copy these answers word for word, as examiners are on the lookout for memorised answers, and will give you lower scores if you use them.

We are sure that you will disagree with many of the statements in the answers. Good! We are happy that you disagree, because that will make you develop your own answers and also think more about the topics and questions.

The best way to use this book is to look at the topics where you feel you lack ideas and vocabulary for the IELTS speaking module. Use the sample answers to get you started on the topic. Most topics are included in Parts 1, 2 and 3. At the same time, notice the different styles of questions, in particular that the part 1 questions are relatively easy and factual, whereas the part 3 questions often involve opinions and personal ideas.

Good luck preparing for the speaking module!

Acknowledgements

First of all, we would like to thank Mark Griffiths for writing the preface to this book and providing the questions from his recently published book on the IELTS Speaking Module.

We would also like to thank our colleagues at New Channel, particularly Hu Min, for his suggestions and guidance, and Cai Qing for help with the design of the book.

Nick Stirk

前 言

本书搜集的考题与本系列丛书中《雅思考试(IELTS)口语突破》的考题相同。每个考题都提供了参考答案，但要记住的是，对于本书中的考题以及实际雅思考试中的口语部分，答案可以千变万化。与大家的想法相反，任何考题都不可能有所谓的正确答案。

雅思口语与雅思写作一样，考官希望你能给出理由支持你的想法、阐明你的观点。之所以要阐明你的观点，其主要原因是：你得向考官展示你的词汇和语法知识，同时让你有机会使用连接词，证明你说话有条理。

参考答案提供了一些有用的词汇，你在回答问题时可以而且应该使用。千万不要一字不落地背这些答案，考官们会特别注意你是否在背答案，如果是，你的成绩会大打折扣。

可以肯定的是，你会不同意参考答案中的许多观点。太好啦！我们很高兴你有不同意见，因为这样会迫使你阐明自己的观点，同时对你碰到的考题做更多的思考。

使用本书的最佳办法是，你觉得自己对雅思口语中哪些考题比较没有把握，就在本书当中重点学习相关内容，让参考答案为你起到提示作用。大多数考题都在第 1、2、3 部分，大家要注意提问的方式各有不同，尤其要注意的是，第 1 部分的提问相对说来不仅容易而且与你的真实情况有关，第 3 部分的提问则经常涉及个人的想法和观点。

祝大家准备充分、心想事成！

鸣 谢

首先我们要感谢 Mark Griffiths 为本书作序并从他最近出版的新书《雅思考试(IELTS)口语突破》中提供考题。

我们还要感谢新航道的同事们为本书提供宝贵建议和指导，尤其是胡敏先生。另外还要感谢蔡箐女士为本书的设计提供了帮助。

Nick Stirk

Contents
目　录

Part One Topics　口试第一阶段常见话题

Part Two Topics 口试第二阶段常见话题

Part Three Topics 口试第三阶段常见话题

Part One Topics

口试第一阶段
常见话题

Ages 年龄

1. When do people (usually) get married in your country?

"When they are in their 20's. People marry later now. This is certainly true in cities. This trend will continue in the next few years. People are putting their careers first. More people are choosing to study longer and leave marriage until they have graduated and found a good job."

2. When do people usually learn to drive in your country?

"In their mid-20's. It is becoming more common to learn earlier. I think that learning at an early age can be dangerous. Younger people are often not careful drivers."

3. At what age(s) can people legally smoke, buy alcohol, and get married?

"For smoking and drinking alcohol, I'm not sure. I often see kids buying cigarettes or bottles of beer and spirits. Maybe they are buying them for themselves or for their parents. I think the legal age should be 18 for this. Getting married? I don't know the age for sure, but I think it's 22 or 24. It might be different for men and for women."

4. At what age do people usually retire from work?

"I heard that the age is 60 for men and 55 for women, but I'm really not sure. Many people retire early or are retired by their companies. This means that they stay at home, but still receive money from the company. This system will not exist in the future, because it is not economical for the company."

5. What could you do when you were younger that you cannot do now?

"Sports mainly. I'm still fit, but when I was younger, I could run a mile in five minutes. I used to be a fast swimmer, too. Now, I only go swimming once every two weeks, so I can't be as good as I was before."

6. How do you think your life will be different when you are retired?

"I'm sure that life will be more relaxing. It might be too relaxing and I'll get bored. At the moment, I want to work part-time when I'm old. I'm not sure I'll feel that way when I retire."

Agriculture 农业

1. What are the main agricultural products in your region / country?

"I live in Hainan. There are many agricultural products, such as rubber, fruits, and vegetables. A lot of melons are grown there. Some of these agricultural products have been grown in Hainan for a long time. Others are new."

2. Do many people work on farms in your region / country?

"In China, many people work in agriculture. People often do not want to work on the land for low pay. Farm workers can earn more in the cities. They cannot get good jobs, so when they arrive in the cities, they get low-paid work in construction or beg for money."

3. Do students often work on farms during their holidays?

"Yes, in the countryside. Parents in the cities want their children to do schoolwork during the school holidays. In China, people that get their money from farming are often poor. The children often work to increase the family income. In cities they have more money, so parents want their kids to do schoolwork."

4. Is farm work well paid in your region / country?

"No. Farm workers often earn less than 1000 yuan a month. Some farmers make a good salary, for example farmers near cities. They can sell products easily. Compared to other people in the countryside, they do well, but compared to city people, their incomes are still low."

5. How important is farming in your region / country?

"In Hainan, farming is quite important, but not as important as the tourist industry. Farming is quite important everywhere in China. In Inner Mongolia, animals are important, but in central China, rice is. In Hainan, fruit and vegetables are the main focus, but rubber plantations are becoming more common."

Ambitions 理想

1. What is your main ambition in life?

"My ambition in life is to stay healthy. If you are healthy, you can work and enjoy yourself in your free time. I keep fit. I eat a balanced diet. I am careful on the streets. Traffic accidents are a cause of injury."

2. Do you think you will achieve your ambition?

"I think so. It is very challenging, but I like challenges, so I am sure I will be successful and achieve my ambition in the future."

3. Do you think that you are an ambitious person?

"Yes. I want to be successful. I want to be very famous and very rich. I want money to buy a big house and travel to foreign countries. I want as much money as Bill Gates! I want to be a 'big boss' and tell people what to do."

4. Are your friends / family members ambitious?

"The people in my family are very ambitious. They are successful and I want to be successful, too. Many of my friends are ambitious. However, I don't think my friends are more ambitious than me."

5. Is it always good to be ambitious?

"Not always. Maybe ambitious people will be selfish. I think that ambition is a good thing. If people are ambitious, they help society, not only the individual. However, some ambitious people will not do this."

6. What do you see yourself doing in 5 / 10 / 20 years' time?

"I'll probably be doing the same thing as now. I hope I'll have a higher position in a large company. My life will be better. I will have a job in a company where I can improve myself."

Animals 动物

1. Do you have a pet?

"I have a pet snake. My friends are surprised that I haven't given her a name, but what's the point? She's never going to respond to it! She's a boa constrictor, so she is not poisonous. In fact, she's not really very dangerous as long as she's well fed. She eats any small mammals. My friends often think it's cruel to feed them to her, but it's just natural."

2. Do people in your country often keep pets?

"A lot of people keep dogs. They tell me that they keep them for protection. Fine, but keep them away from my snake, or the 'protection' might become 'lunch'. Other people keep dogs for company. Dogs are happy to sit next to their owner or go for a walk. They're not difficult to look after."

3. Are wild animals protected in your region / country?

"There are laws to protect wild animals. People sometimes hunt wild animals for their fur, to eat, or to use in medicine. Wild animals need protection. If they are dangerous, they should be dealt with."

4. Do you often visit zoos or wildlife parks?

"I go once a year with my daughter. She likes watching the animals. She learns a lot about the animals at the zoo. I don't want her to see animals trapped in small cages. I take her to places where the environment is natural."

5. Which is your favourite animal?

"I like snakes. I like the way they move. They can be difficult to look after, though."

6. Are there any animals that you are afraid of?

"I'm afraid of spiders. I think it's all those legs! Small ones are OK, but I'm afraid of the big ones with the hairy legs."

Examiners have access to these model answers.
If you copy any of them, you could get a very low score in the IELTS test.

Birthdays 生日

1. How do people celebrate birthdays in your culture?

"People often have a party. It depends on the age of the person. Children have some friends join them at home. Older people prefer a meal at a restaurant. Of course, a birthday cake is traditional, with the number of candles equal to the age of the birthday boy or girl. Many adults don't like to be reminded of this though!"

2. Do people in your family celebrate birthdays in different ways?

"We're typical. The children will have a party at home. The adults go out to a nice restaurant. We always eat Chinese food."

3. Tell me a little about the best birthday celebration you have been to.

"I think my father's 70th birthday was the best one. The weather was nice. We had tables outside with food and drink. We ate, drank, and talked all afternoon. Many of my father's friends, relatives and colleagues came with presents."

4. What was the best birthday present you ever received?

"My father bought me a mobile phone for my 10th birthday. It was made by British Telecom. All my friends had mobile phones so we could communicate with each other."

5. What kind of presents do you get people for their birthdays?

"I usually buy something which is both inexpensive and practical for my colleagues. However, I like to splash out (= spend a lot of money) on gifts for my wife, in order to show her how much I love her. I often go shopping for gifts at Guo Mao which has a great selection of shops."

6. What would you do with a birthday gift you didn't like?

"If I received a gift which I didn't like, such as a CD by an artist I hated, I would probably just bury it in my collection. I suppose I could give it to someone who liked that music, but what if the person who gave me the CD came to visit and said 'Play that CD I gave you for Christmas'?"

Books 书籍

1. How often do you read books?

"I love reading political thrillers and Sherlock Holmes detective stories. I usually read them in bed every evening. I read them very quickly."

2. Who is your favourite writer?

"My favourite writer is the American novelist, Tom Clancy, who writes political thrillers. His books are always really thick – usually well over 1000 pages long! A few of his books have been made into films. His first bestseller was 'The Hunt for Red October'. The film version starred Sean Connery, best known for his role as the first James Bond."

3. When do you usually like to read?

"Many people like to read a newspaper or magazine when they have a little free time, such as when they are travelling on the subway. I know many people who like reading a book in bed."

4. Do you read more for pleasure or to get information?

"I mainly read for pleasure – just to relax. I read newspapers and articles on the Internet for information. I like to know what is happening in the world. Many people say that the world is getting smaller, thanks to modern technology, yet still have no idea what is happening around them."

5. Do you often buy books as gifts for family or friends?

"Yes, I do, because most of my friends like reading, too. My son and my daughter also read a lot, but other people in my family don't, so I buy them clothes or CD's."

6. Would you like to write a book one day?

"Actually, I've already written two textbooks and a novel. I'm planning another novel and writing another textbook at the moment. The textbooks were quite successful, but the novel wasn't. It was nice to earn royalties from the books, but I wrote them more for my own sense of achievement, rather than the cash."

Clothes 衣服

1. Do you wear different clothes for work and for leisure?

"Most people do, but I don't. In my office, I don't have to wear formal clothes. As long as I look OK and my clothes are clean, my boss doesn't mind. I often have to work outside, so a suit is not a good idea. Most of the time, I wear a skirt, a blouse, and comfortable shoes."

2. Which kind of clothes do you prefer to wear?

"I prefer to wear smart casual clothes. I like to wear plain clothes without bright colours. I have a few bright beach shirts, which I wear to bars. I like clothes that are comfortable to wear, especially in hot weather. Sometimes, I must wear a suit. Then I don't feel comfortable."

3. Do you have a special set of clothes for special occasions?

"I have a very expensive Armani suit, which I bought a year ago in London. I'm an ugly middle-aged guy, but when I wear this suit, I get some admiring looks from ladies. I wear it to important meetings (with new clients for instance) and dinner parties. It's a black silk suit."

4. Do you pay more attention to the quality of clothes you buy or to the price?

"I used to choose according to the price a few years ago, but now I have a higher income and can buy better clothes. I prefer to buy clothes in Europe, because I like the styles and the choice. I usually go to the city centre and look at the clothes in several shops before buying."

5. How important do you think it is to be fashionable?

"I think it's very important. People care what you look like. I go to fashion shows to see the latest clothes and buy them direct from the designers. In China, people like people who look modern and cool. They respect them. If you are fashionable, you must be rich, so people will like you."

Computers 计算机

1. How often do you use a computer?

"I hardly ever use them. I'm a driver, so I don't need them at work. Sometimes, I check my email, read a news article, or play a computer game. My son uses them a lot. He likes surfing on the Internet very much."

2. Which websites do you often visit on the Internet?

"I go to 'Yahoo!' to check my email and sometimes read the news. I can use that page to search on the Internet. I often visit websites associated with films and TV series. I also like to visit English teaching websites like 'www. in2english.com'. Every evening, I like to visit www.purple.com because I find it very relaxing to look at this colour on the screen for a few minutes before going to bed. The website is just a purple screen – there is nothing else there."

3. In what ways do people use computers in your country?

"I think that most people use computers like me. Or do I use computers in the same way they do? Computers are often used by the police to control traffic lights, by banks to keep track of accounts, and by scientists to record data from experiments."

4. How "computer literate" are you?

"I'm pretty good at using computers, but I have never taken a computer course. My job doesn't involve using a computer. I can use common programmes, like Word and Excel, but nothing too complicated."

5. How much have computers changed your life?

"Directly, not very much. I don't use them very often. I use Internet banking to pay household bills, transfer money to foreign accounts, and exchange currencies. Computers have changed my life indirectly, for example computers help us to see what the weather will be like. I often need to check the weather forecast, because I work outside."

Crime 犯罪

1. Is crime a problem in your city / region / country?

"Yes, it's a big problem. Violent crime is decreasing, but the media likes those stories. Theft is increasing. I think many people are prepared to get rich by any possible means."

2. Which kind of crime do you think is the biggest problem in your region?

"I think theft. People steal from other people and from companies. They want to get rich quickly. People need to be more careful about theft, but it's a crime that will never be eliminated."

3. Have you ever witnessed a crime?

"Once, I saw a young man grab a ladies handbag and run off with it. He did it in a crowded shopping area. He didn't get very far, though. Two men caught him and held him to the ground until a policeman arrived. It was exciting, but only lasted a few seconds. The young thief was certainly not too happy – he could be heard swearing at the two men who caught him. Actually, that part was quite funny! The old lady was very grateful to the men, but they didn't accept a reward. They were just happy to be good citizens."

4. What do you do to protect yourself and your home from thieves?

"I'm very careful to lock all the windows in my home before going out. I do this even if it's a hot day, so the house can get very hot inside. If I use my bicycle, I use a bicycle chain. I don't carry a wallet, but that's partly because of pickpockets, partly because I'm afraid I'll just lose it."

5. Do you often read newspaper articles about crime?

"There are lots of stories about crime in newspapers, but I hardly ever read them. Crime is an everyday thing. If the crime isn't unusual, it doesn't get my attention. Sometimes, the crimes are funny!"

Cultural Events and Entertainment
文化活动与娱乐

1. Do you often go to the theatre / the opera / concerts / exhibitions?

"I used to go to the opera and theatre occasionally, but I haven't been for a few years now. It's quite expensive and you can buy performances on DVD quite easily and more cheaply. I go to see live music quite often. I go to see live music at various bars in Beijing. I don't really mind what kind of music it is, as long as it's lively and the performers put on a good show."

2. Tell me a little about the last time you went to a cultural event.

"Last weekend, I went to see a punk-rock band at a bar in Beijing. The four members of the group were all girls. They looked so cool with their clothes and make-up. The music was loud and energetic. They sang in Chinese, so I didn't understand the lyrics. Most of the audience were, like me, dressed in normal casual clothes. Many people in the crowd, especially the young men, looked surprised. I don't think that they expect Chinese girls to look and act like this!"

3. What kinds of cultural events do people like to go to in your city / region?

"I think that concerts and live music in bars are most popular. There are several minorities in my city, so there are often cultural events associated with their festivals."

4. Is it expensive to go to such events?

"Going to the opera in Britain is quite expensive. I doubt that you can get tickets for less than £20. That would be for tickets right at the back of the opera hall. Many of the expensive tickets (perhaps £200 for the best seats!) are bought by companies who want to impress clients."

5. Do you think that such events are important in people's lives?

"Yes, certainly. People like to be entertained – and there's no shortage of people willing to try and entertain them! I think people love their city more because it has something happening. People can relax and enjoy themselves."

6. Have you ever participated in a cultural event (or exhibition)?

"Last year, my boss asked me to be on the company stand at an exhibition. I thought it would be boring, but it wasn't that bad. I was happy to give out leaflets with information about our company and its products, and answer people's questions."

Daily Routines 日常生活

1. When do you usually get up / go to bed?

"On workdays, I get up at 6:30, which is probably earlier than most of my colleagues, simply because I live further from the office than anyone else. The time that I go to bed depends on if I'm having a quiet evening, reading a novel, or going out with friends, but is normally about midnight."

2. Are your weekday and weekend routines different?

"They certainly are! During the week, I work. Then I go home to eat dinner or eat at a restaurant. After dinner, I often go out to a bar. On Saturdays, I do all the housework (cleaning and washing) and shopping. In the evening, I go out with friends. On Sundays, I don't really have a routine. What I do depends on the weather. If it's a nice day, I go out, either somewhere in the city or to the countryside. If not, I usually stay at home and watch a film or read a book. Then I go out with friends in the evening again."

3.What would you like to change about your weekday / workday routine?

"I would like to start work earlier, before the rush hour. Then I could leave the office earlier and have more free time in the late afternoons and evenings."

4. At what times do you usually eat your meals?

"I eat breakfast at seven o'clock, lunch at midday, and dinner at seven in the evening. That's the same for weekdays and weekends, unless there's something special which changes my routine. I eat breakfast at home and lunch at a restaurant near my office. Dinner could be either at home or a restaurant."

5. What is your favourite part of the day?

"I like the evenings, because I can relax after work or go out with friends and have some fun. I think most people are happy when their workday is over and they can do what they like to do."

6. What is the worst part of your day?

"For me, the worst part of the day is the early afternoon, just after lunch. Like many people, I feel a little tired after lunch (particularly a big one!) and need a nap. Unfortunately, I have to continue working, which can be hard. I guess I could try eating a smaller lunch, but then I'd be hungry later in the afternoon."

Examiners have access to these model answers.
If you copy any of them, you could get a very low score in the IELTS test.

Education 教育

1. What was your favourite subject at secondary (high) school?

"I liked history most of all. I've always been interested in what happened in the past, finding out why it happened, and what it can teach us for the future. I had four lessons per week. In the early years of my secondary education, we didn't examine the events in too much detail, but in later years we did, which I found much more interesting and useful. I found the subject most useful because I could see how the modern world had been shaped by these events."

2. How many subjects do secondary (high) school students usually have to study?

"In Britain, students usually study about twelve subjects between the ages of 11 and 14, then nine or ten between the ages of 14 and 16. Some of these can be selected by the student. If they continue their education, they choose two to five subjects to study for the next two years."

3. Do many secondary (high) school students go on to university?

"About 50% of the Chinese students who want to go to universities are successful. This number is much higher in Beijing and Shanghai – about 80%. They believe that a university education will help them in the job market later. Most young people find a job. They are not as good at schoolwork and think work experience is important. Others decide to go abroad to study for a short period."

4. Is education in your country free?

"Education is free for students up to the age of 18, though parents have to pay for some practical subjects (e.g. buying a musical instrument). Chinese students pay to go to university and pay the costs of materials and accommodation."

5. Do students have to wear uniforms at schools in your country?

"Most British schools require students to wear a uniform, but the policy is decided independently by each school. Personally, I think it's a good idea, but most kids would prefer to wear what they like."

Family 家庭

1. Do you live alone or with other people?

"I live with my wife and two kids in a big house just outside the second ring road. After finishing university, I lived alone for a few years, before getting married. I preferred living alone, because I could do what I liked and could keep my lifestyle private. Of course, eventually I had to make a choice – get married or live alone. I think I made the right choice!"

2. What jobs do the people in your immediate family do?

"My father works as an editor for a medium-sized publishing company. He's been working there for many years and seems happy to stay there until he retires. My mother is a paediatrician – a doctor specializing in children's medicine. She works in a local hospital. My father works regular hours, Monday to Friday, with overtime at busy periods. My mother, on the other hand, works different shifts each month, which is quite stressful."

3. What kind of things do you and your family do together?

"We sometimes watch TV together, if there's something we all like. At the weekends, we often get in the car and go out into the countryside to visit a place of historical or cultural significance. My brother doesn't like these trips too much and often complains. So, sometimes we let him go out with his friends instead."

4. Who does the housework in your home?

"As I live alone, the answer to that question is 'me'. My friends tell me that I should get a housemaid, but I'm quite happy doing the housework myself. I used to do it for pocket money when I was a child."

5. Do you have a large extended family?

"The members of my extended family live in most of the English speaking countries of the world. I have aunts, uncles and cousins in Canada, the USA, Australia, New Zealand, and South Africa. A few still live in Britain. Obviously, I see them more often than the others. Every five years or so, we have a big family get together in London, which is paid for by the richer members of the extended family."

Festivals 节日

1. Do you often celebrate festivals in your culture / country?

"Yes. The main festivals we celebrate are the Spring Festival, Tomb Sweeping Day, Workers' Day, National Day and the Mid-Autumn Festival. People like to spend festivals with their families. As a result, it is difficult to travel at the beginning and end of the Spring Festival, Workers' Day holiday and National Day holiday."

2. Do these festivals have special meanings?

"Spring Festival celebrates the beginning of the Chinese year. Workers' Day honours workers. National Day celebrates the founding of the People's Republic of China in 1949. Tomb Sweeping Day is when people remember their ancestors and visit their tombs or shrines."

3. Are there any festivals special to your city or region?

"No, there are none that I can think of."

4. What special things do people do during festivals?

"People often dance in their ethnic costumes, sing traditional songs, and play traditional music. Other people visit shrines and light candles or incense there. Others participate in parades on the streets."

5. Which is your favourite festival?

"I like Valentine's Day. It is a romantic day for lovers. You give your boyfriend or girlfriend a small gift to show your love. The Chinese Lover's Day is on the seventh day of the seventh month."

6. Do you celebrate any foreign festivals?

"In Britain, it is becoming common to recognize the festivals that ethnic minorities celebrate. What usually happens is that the ethnic minority celebrates its festival, but people from other cultures watch and join in the festive mood. Chinese New Year is a good example of this, because it is something that you can enjoy watching, even if you don't really know much about it. People set off fireworks and firecrackers, or do lion and dragon dances."

Films / Movies 电影

1. What kinds of films / movies do you like to watch?

"I like horror movies, like 'The Ring' and 'Frankenstein'. I actually like being scared! It's sometimes funny to watch a horror film with a person who gets scared more easily than I do. The use of special effects can make modern horror films terrifying, but some older horror films managed to do this without the effects."

2. Are these kinds of films / movies popular in your country?

"I think that a lot of young people like them, but older people prefer films which focus on relationships between people, not on action. I think men enjoy horror films more than women. Perhaps they like to show that they are not scared."

3. Which was the best film / movie you ever saw?

"Perhaps the best film I ever saw was Forrest Gump. It is one of the few movies that I have watched more than once. It shows that success is a mixture of luck and hard work. It made me laugh and cry. Many of my students have seen this film and some even gave themselves the English name Forrest after the star."

4. Who is your favourite actor / actress?

"My favourite actress is Joan Chen. She was born in Shanghai, in China, in 1961. However, she has spent most of her life in the United States. When she was 14, she was selected to study at the Shanghai Film Academy. Four years later she won the Golden Rooster award for Best Actress for her role in the film 'Little flower'. When she was 20, she went to the United Sates. She appeared in the film 'Tai-Pan', but her first starring role in the US was in 'The Last Emperor'. She played the Empress. In 1998, she produced and directed the film 'Xiu Xiu: the Sent Down Girl' set during the Cultural Revolution."

5. What kind of roles does he / she usually play?

"Joan Chen is most famous for her role as the Empress in 'The Last Emperor', but more recently, she has played the role of villain in a few films."

6. Would you like to be a film star?

"I'd love to make comedies. I enjoy telling jokes, especially naughty ones! My friends say that I am very good at making funny faces and voices, so I think that I'd make a pretty good comedy actor."

Food and Cooking 饮食

1. What is your favourite food or meal?

"Like many British people, I love fish 'n' chips. I used to run to the fish 'n' chip shop to get food for the whole family. If it was a nice summer evening, I would sit and eat them outside. In Britain, fish 'n' chips are traditionally sprinkled with salt and vinegar, then wrapped in newspaper in the shop. I suppose that they are not so healthy, but no-one seems to mind about that. Now, there's a fish 'n' chip shop in Beijing, too! I can eat fish 'n' chips every day!"

2. Do you like to cook?

"I like cooking and can cook several dishes well. I can cook Italian and British food. They are not very difficult to make. I cannot cook Chinese food, but I am taking a Chinese cookery class at the Guangzhou School of Culture."

3. Who usually cooks in your home?

"I live alone, so I cook for myself. My kitchen is modern, so I can cook complicated dishes. I don't cook every day. Sometimes, I go to a restaurant near my home, especially if I am tired after work. There is a Korean restaurant. It is small and a little dirty, but the food is great."

4. Is food expensive in your country?

"Most food is cheap here but obviously fresh fruit and vegetables are more expensive in the city than in the countryside. In the street you can bargain over the price but in supermarkets the price is fixed although the quality may be better. Sometimes I will buy a lot of fruit because it is in season and cheap."

5. Are there any kinds of food that you do not like?

"I'm a vegetarian, so I don't eat any food that contains animal products. I just don't like the taste of meat. I cook for myself, so I don't worry about animal products getting into my food. However, I must be careful at restaurants."

Friends 朋友

1. Do you often spend time with friends?

"I go out with my friends most evenings. We like to go to a bar near where we work. We drink a few beers, talk about our lives, and play pool. Most of my friends are men, but sometimes a woman joins us. We go out four or five times a week for about two or three hours each time."

2. Did you meet most of your friends through school / work?

"I met most of my friends through work. I still have some old friends from university. We don't see each other very often now. I hardly ever use the Internet, so I haven't met anyone that way."

3. Do you and your friends have similar hobbies and interests?

"We all like going out, so we often enjoy the nightlife in this city. Each of us has some other interests, such as skiing or diving. We don't do those activities together, but we tell each other about them when we meet."

4. Do you spend more of your free time with friends or with family?

"I spend much more time with my friends. My family lives nearby, but I prefer to be with friends. In my country, family members usually have different interests, so they don't spend much time together."

5. Do you have any friends who live / work far away from you?

"I have taught English in many different countries, so obviously I have many friends who live far, far away from me now. I don't chat with them on the phone or even online, because of the time difference. When I am free in the evening, they are at work. When they finish work, I am asleep. We do send emails to each other, but not very regularly."

Examiners have access to these model answers.
If you copy any of them, you could get a very low score in the IELTS test.

Games 游戏

1. Do you often play games with your family or friends?

"I like playing hide-and-seek with my friends. It's a simple game and the number of people isn't important. You can play with two people or ten people. I sometimes play Chinese chess with my grandfather. He usually wins."

2. Which is your favourite game?

"My favourite game is 'Twister'. You need at least 2 people to play (5 or 6 is better!) and another person to be the judge. There is a white cloth on the floor with spots of different colours (red, yellow, green and blue). The judge spins a special wheel, which indicates which colour spots people must put their hands or feet on. If a person cannot put their hand or foot on the spots of given colour, if they fall over, or if they push another person they are out. It's a funny game, because people get twisted around each other in strange positions."

3. Does the winner get a prize?

"You can give a small prize if you want (like chocolate), but we usually don't. Prizes are certainly a good idea for children's games and I think many adults secretly like to receive prizes, too."

4. Are these games popular in your country?

"I think that hide-and-seek is popular, but Twister isn't. Most people have heard of Twister, but don't play it."

5. Do people in your family prefer different games?

"My sister likes to play computer games, but my mother prefers Mah Jong. It could be that younger people are more technologically minded, whereas older people prefer more traditional Chinese games."

Going Abroad Long-term 出国计划

1. Why are you planning to spend a period of time abroad?

"I'm going abroad to travel. I think I should visit many different countries now, before I start a career. I want to visit the USA, Italy, Egypt and India, before I return to China. I will spend several weeks in each country."

2. How long do you plan to be abroad?

"Probably about three months, maybe longer if I have fun and enough money. I would like to travel for about a year!"

3. How have your family and friends supported you in this?

"My parents are supporting me with money and a friend who travelled abroad is giving me advice about travel, places to visit, finding accommodation, and how to meet people."

4. How *exactly* will you benefit from this experience?

"The course in genetics at Cambridge will be more useful than studying anywhere in China because they have the best research labs. The course in human genetics is taught by Professor Harding, the world's leading expert in this field. I'm sure these things will help me learn a lot."

5. What problems do you think you may have abroad?

"I don't think I'll have any problems abroad. I've been abroad before, so I know I have no problem with homesickness. Language shouldn't be a problem as I speak English and French very well. I'll need to be careful with money – travelling can be expensive."

6. How do you think the country you live in will be different to China?

"There are many ways it will be different. The food will be different, but I have been to western restaurants, so that will not be a big problem. The climate will be wetter and colder than in Beijing. Westerners are usually more direct than Chinese people. Young people often go to bars and clubs in Western countries. There is more student participation in classes."

Examiners have access to these model answers.
If you copy any of them, you could get a very low score in the IELTS test.

Health and Fitness 健康和健身

1. Do you try to keep fit?

"I think that I keep quite fit. I like to go jogging most mornings, but just along the canal behind my home. Luckily, there is a well-equipped fitness centre near my office, which means I can drop in before or after work. I also like to go to a hotel swimming pool at the weekends."

2. Have you ever been a member of a fitness club?

"Yes, as I said, there is one near my office. I joined about 2 years ago, when I first came to Beijing. They have several machines for jogging and lifting weights. It's a small club, so it can be crowded. The people there are very helpful. It costs $50 per month."

3. Do you think you have a healthy diet?

"Not really. I go to fast food places almost every day, and I eat too much chocolate. I don't exercise and now I'm really fat."

4. How do you think you could improve your health?

"I think I could do a few things. I could go jogging in the mornings. I could go to the fitness centre near my office before or after work. I could also go swimming at the lake near my home at weekends."

5. Do you often visit a doctor (for a check up)?

"I only go to the doctor when there is a serious problem with my health. For small problems, I go to the pharmacy and get some medicine. It's not very expensive and saves time."

6. Do you have to pay to visit a doctor in your country?

"In the United States, you pay to visit a doctor, but your insurance company will probably cover the cost. It's very expensive. You sometimes pay $100 just to see the doctor! But the service is usually very good."

Hobbies and Interests 爱好和兴趣

1. What do you do in your free time?

"I like reading novels and listening to music. I read detective novels by Sir Arthur Conan Doyle and political thrillers by Tom Clancy. I like American country music by John Denver and Dolly Parton. Sometimes I play tennis with my friends. We play at the tennis courts next to my office."

2. Did you have other hobbies / interests when you were younger?

"I used to go horse riding and collect stamps when I was a child. I gave up horse riding because it was too expensive and I gave up stamp collecting because it took up too much time."

3. What does your husband / wife / mother / father do in his / her free time?

"My husband plays Mah Jong with his friends two or three evenings a week. My parents are retired and their hobby is hiking in the countryside near their home. They really love nature."

4. Are these activities popular in your country?

"Yes, these free time activities are very popular, especially with older people who have more time to relax. Younger people prefer more 'active' hobbies, maybe because they have more energy."

5. If you had more free time, what would you do?

"If I had more free time, I would write a book about my travel experiences. I would only include short, funny stories from my travels, particularly those which show how differences in culture and language can cause hilarious situations. It would probably take a long time to write, but in the end I might make some money from the book. It would also be nice to see my name in bookshops and think that people were reading my experiences."

Holidays / Vacations 假日

1. How often do you go on holiday?

"I usually go on holiday twice a year to Hainan, which is an island at the southern tip of China. I love sunbathing on the beach and drinking cocktails. My favourite hotel is right on the beach where it is reasonably peaceful."

2. Where do you usually go? / Tell me more about where you usually go.

"I usually go to places near Urumuqi. There are many interesting places outside the city. I like to relax and take photographs at the Heavenly Lake and Southern Pastures. Many people like to have their photographs taken here, so maybe I could do this as a job, not just a hobby."

3. Who do you prefer to go with?

"I prefer to go with friends who are interested in photography and history, because the areas outside Urumuqi are historical and beautiful, especially the Heavenly Lake and Southern Pastures. We like to sit down in the countryside, have a picnic and chat on a beautiful sunny afternoon."

4. What do you like to do on holiday?

"I like to take photographs and visit interesting historical places. Sometimes, I like to relax on a beach or in a bar. I don't like to use too much energy on holiday. It's a time for relaxing."

5. If you could go to any foreign country for a holiday, where would you go?

"I would like to go to Japan with my girlfriend. She wants to pick up some fashion ideas in Tokyo whilst I'm interested in climbing Mount Fuji. Some people might think it's strange to go on holiday with someone then not spend all the time together. The thing is that we both enjoy photography, but she prefers fashion photography whereas I prefer photographing the scenery."

Hotels 旅馆

1. Have you ever stayed in a really nice / expensive hotel?

"I've never stayed in a hotel, because I'm still at high school, so I have no real reason to travel much. Whenever I go on holiday with my parents, we stay with relatives. However, a classmate recently went to Moscow and stayed at the 5-star Lenin Hotel. She said that it had two swimming pools and sauna, which she used often, because they were free for guests. She also told me that the hotel had a revolving restaurant on the top floor, which gave wonderful views of Red Square. The restaurant served Russian and international specialties. Although the hotel and facilities were fine, she didn't think that the service was very good. In particular, the waiters were extremely slow, she said."

2. Do people in your country often stay in hotels?

"Hotels are too expensive for most people. Anyway, not many people travel. Businessmen often stay in hotels. Their companies pay, so the price isn't so important."

3. What services and facilities are usually available in hotels in your country?

"A 5-star hotel has a TV in every room, a bar, a swimming pool, a beauty salon, a restaurant, currency exchange, safety deposit box, post office services, laundry service, shoe-shine service, a hairdryer, a trouser press, air conditioning, wake up call service, and a sauna."

4. How much does a hotel room in your town / city cost per night?

"A 5-star hotel costs around $100 a night, but a 2-star hotel only costs about $20. There are many hotels in my city, so it's easy to make a suitable choice."

5. What factors are important when selecting a hotel?

"There are many things to think about – price, where it is relative to the places you want to visit, transport, service, the hotel restaurants, and facilities."

Languages 语言

1. Do many foreigners speak your native language?

"Chinese is becoming a useful language because trade with China is increasing. Many foreigners come to China to study Chinese, at the Beijing Language and Culture University, for example. More foreigners who are not ethnically Chinese are studying Chinese, even at secondary schools. Also, hundreds of thousands of foreigners live and work in China and learn the language during their stays. Most foreigners who study Chinese don't speak very well. If they study at BLCU or another university, they often speak it very well."

2. How important is your native language in the world today?

"I think Chinese is very important in East Asia, but not very important in the rest of the world. Chinese is one of the official languages of the United Nations, but I think that is simply thanks to the fact that China has such a large population. English is used as the primary language in many countries. Chinese is not. Still, Chinese is useful because countries want to trade with China."

3. How long have you been studying English?

"I have studied English for 5 years. I began at university. Now, I use it at work every day."

4. Do you think your native language is easier than English?

"I think Chinese grammar and pronunciation is easier, but reading and writing in English is easier for students."

5. What other languages can you speak?

"I speak fairly good Russian. It's quite hard to learn for three reasons, in my experience. First, there's the alphabet, which is written differently to English. Then there's the pronunciation. Sometimes it sounds to me like the words are all mixed up. The third and biggest problem, at least for me, is the grammar. There are so many rules!"

The Media 媒体

1. How do you get the latest news?

"I usually get the news from the radio. I think it is fast, reliable, and a radio is cheap to use. You can listen to the radio when you are doing something else, like housework."

2. Do many people in your country listen to the radio?

"I think that they prefer other ways of getting the news. The great thing about the radio is that you can just leave it on while you do other things, like household chores. You don't need to look at it, like you do with TV, the Internet, or newspapers. Radio stations get the news quite quickly – even live from the scene. Radios are cheap to buy and easy to use, but they aren't modern enough for a lot of people who prefer to use the Internet."

3. What kinds of news stories are usually reported on TV in your country?

"They usually report political events, business, sport, domestic news, foreign affairs, weather, disasters, crime, exhibitions, wars, and people's successes. Political events are usually regarded as the most important. They are shown nearly every day, with pictures showing China's leaders."

4. What non-news items can be found in newspapers in your country?

"In newspapers, we can find cartoons, jokes, competitions, reviews of products, and advertisements. I don't like them very much. The reviews are really just advertisements. Some of my friends really believe them! I often enter the competitions and sometimes win prizes."

5. Do you pay more attention to local, national, or international news?

"I pay attention to the local news most. National and international news doesn't mean anything to me. I want to know what is happening in my local area. I often discuss these issues with other people."

Music 音乐

1. What kind(s) of music do you like?

"When I was a kid, I used to like rock music. Now, I prefer techno music, because I find it better to dance to. I've never liked folk or country music. It's just too slow for me. I like fast, energetic music."

2. Can you play a musical instrument?

"I can play the er hu, a traditional Chinese musical instrument. In China, some students learn to play it at school. I like it and I'm very good at it. I play it at concerts in my hometown during festivals."

3. Do your friends and family have different musical tastes to you?

"My friends like the same music as me. We often go to clubs to listen to it. My parents prefer er hu music. I don't like it."

4. Who is your favourite singer or musician?

"My favourite singer is the rap artist A1. He's from the United States. He went to jail for drug-dealing when he was young. He soon found he could make money from rap and not have problems with the police. He made his first album, 'Pig in the Middle', in 1998. It sold over 100,000 copies. He's famous in the United States, but not in other countries."

5. Have you ever been to one of their performances or seen one on TV?

"Yes, I saw him at a concert in Los Angeles, two years ago. It was expensive–$50 – but I liked the concert very much. Of course, I have seen his music videos on TV many times."

6. What do you think of karaoke?

"This is very popular in Eastern Asia – much more than in the West. I like watching other people sing, but I don't sing myself."

Names 名字

1. Is your given name / family name a common one in your country?

"Yes, my surname is Wang which is commonly used in China. I have some classmates with the same name but we are not related in any way. I am always meeting strangers who are also called Wang."

2. Do people in your country / culture usually have middle names?

"Many Chinese people have two given names, which is like having a middle name."

3. Does your name mean anything or have a special significance?

"My family name means 'young'. My father gave me my given name because he wanted me to be an ordinary person."

4. Do any (other) people in your family have names with special meanings?

"Yes, my father's name means 'powerful' and my mother's name means 'tender'. However, my mother is the real power in our household!"

5. Would you like to change your name?

"Yes. I don't like my name and want to change it when I finish high school."

6. In your culture, do women change their names when they get married?

"In China, it is not customary for women to change their names, unlike women in Western countries. This is changing slowly."

7. What are the most common names in your country (culture)?

"Over 50% of Chinese people have one of the following family names – Chen, Lin, Huang, Li, Zhang, Wu, Wang, Cai, Liu. The most common given names (and their meanings) are: Wen (culture, writing), Zhi (will, intention, emotions), Yi (cheerful), Ya (elegant), Ming (bright), Hui (smart, wise), Hong (great, wide)."

Places of Interest 风景名胜

1. Which places in your city or province would you suggest a tourist visit?

"I think that people should visit the Potola Palace. It is a monastery in the centre of Lhasa. I'm very lucky, because I can actually see it from my home. People can also visit Mount Everest, the world's highest mountain. I wouldn't suggest that they climb it, but they can visit the base camp."

2. Why are they significant?

"The Potola Palace is significant because it is a historic building with a long history. Mount Everest is the world's highest mountain – a real challenge for mountaineers from all over the world."

3. Do you often visit such places?

"No I don't. It is expensive to take my family with me because of the entrance fee so I only go once or twice a year. Besides I have been many times before so it is no longer so interesting to me. If special friends come to see me then of course I will take them there."

4. What kind of places of interest do you like to visit?

"I like visiting museums such as the military museum in Beijing. You can learn a lot from the exhibits there. My major is history and museums are obviously full of historical information."

5. Do you like to take photographs at places of interest?

"Yes, of course I do. If I am alone I try to get a stranger to take a photo of me standing in front of whatever it is. Later I can look at the photos to remind myself of the happy time I had or I can show them to my friends."

6. Do you often visit places of natural beauty?

"Not very often because I study so much and therefore have very little free time. If I do have a day to spare I like to go to the Summer Palace because it reminds me of my hometown Hangzhou and West Lake. It is so peaceful and lovely there so I can sit beneath a tree by the lakeside and forget all my worries."

Possessions 财产

1. Do you own something which was expensive to buy?

"My house was very expensive. It cost two million RMB. I'm very happy with it. I bought it five years ago. It's in the countryside. The air is clean and the surrounding area is very beautiful."

2. Do people in your country often buy expensive items?

"People often give children a lot of money for Spring Festival. They buy expensive things for people when they get married."

3. Do you own something which was a special gift to you?

"I was given a Walkman by a Japanese friend. We worked together for three months. I use it for listening to English. It cost about $100. It is made by Sony and includes a radio."

4. Do you own any items which are very old?

"I have a few old items. My mother gave me a stamp from 1860, a Ming dynasty vase and a gold ring made in the 1920's before she died."

5. How important are possessions to you?

"I like things that remind me of people or places. Often, they are not useful. Of course, I have a few things that are useful and remind me of places or people. I have a coffee cup from London. I use it in my office. No-one else has one like it, so it shouldn't get used by any other person by mistake."

6. What things do you own which you find particularly useful?

"Yes. I use my Walkman to listen to English. I can listen to it on the subway. Because it has a radio, I don't need to carry any CD's with me, although I usually do carry a few."

Restaurants 饭店

1. Do you often go to restaurants?

"I go to an Indian restaurant once a month with my wife. I go to a Shandong restaurant once a week with my colleagues. I go to a Japanese restaurant three times a year with my mother. The Japanese restaurant is my favourite, but it's very expensive – about 500 RMB for two people, including drinks."

2. What kinds of restaurants are near your home?

"There's a big Beijing Duck restaurant down the street from my home. There's a small Cantonese restaurant round the corner from my home. There's a McDonald's on my university campus."

3. What do you think of fast food restaurants?

"Fast food restaurants are clean, efficient, friendly and bright. However, they are expensive. Many of my friends like them, but I only go there once or twice a week. I often take my homework with me and do it while I'm eating and drinking."

4. How good is the service in restaurants where you live?

"Usually it is very good and I don't have to wait very long to be served or for the food to arrive. If the waiters are slow and their clothes are dirty then I won't go there again even if the food is really good. I think that if I am paying for the meal then the service should be quick and the waiters friendly. At one restaurant which I usually go to the staff all know me and so they look after me really well."

5. Do you prefer restaurant food or "home cooking"?

"My mother would kill me if I said I didn't prefer her cooking! Generally, I do prefer her cooking, but some restaurants have specialties which their chefs cook very, very well. She really likes a Japanese restaurant near her home, so I take her there a few times a year. It's very expensive, but the food is delicious."

Shopping 购物

1. Do you enjoy shopping / window shopping?

"I hate shopping. I do all my shopping online or at the small shops near my home. Online, I can look at the products and buy the ones I like. I actually took part in an experiment to see if I could survive by shopping online with a limited amount of money. I was successful! I still think there are some things I should buy at the shop, like milk and vegetables."

2. Do you usually do your shopping at one place or several different places?

"I shop for clothes at a place round the corner from my home which is owned by a friend, because she gives me a discount and gives me some useful fashion tips. I do food shopping at a few different places, according to what I want to buy."

3. What kinds of shops are there near your home?

"There are several small shops on my street. There is a small shoe shop, specializing in women's shoes. There are two small supermarkets. One is a little more expensive, but has a wider range of products and, most importantly, is open 24 hours a day. Oh, and there's a camera shop. You can get photographs developed there and buy photo albums."

4. Do you pay more attention to quality or to price?

"I always pay more attention to quality. My family is so rich that we don't know what to do with our money. People respect me because I can buy quality things. I always get the best service when I'm shopping, because I have so much money. I only look at the price to make sure I'm spending a lot of money!"

5. Have prices increased a lot recently?

"Electricity prices have increased by 20%. The price of children's clothes has gone up a little. Luckily, the price of oil has dropped a lot recently. This means that prices may drop generally."

Examiners have access to these model answers.
If you copy any of them, you could get a very low score in the IELTS test.

Sports 运动

1. Which sports are popular in your country?

"Table tennis, basketball and football. The Chinese are famous for being the best table tennis players in the world. Table tennis is popular with all kinds of people, but basketball and football are mainly popular with young people. Yao Ming is one of the most famous basketball players in the world."

2. Which sports do you watch?

"I like watching skiing. The skiers are very skillful. They go down the mountain slopes very quickly, but only rarely fall. I watch this sport on TV during the skiing season, but I have never tried it."

3. How often do you play sports?

"I play sports every evening with friends. I play volleyball, rugby and ice-hockey. We play at the sports stadium in the centre of this city. I've played volleyball for many years, but I have only played rugby and ice-hockey since I became friends with a group of foreigners who play these sports."

4. Why do you play sports?

"I mainly play sports to relax and be with my friends. Sports keep me fit, but that's not why I play them."

5. Did you play sports when you were younger?

"I used to play football when I was younger, but now I only have time for a short game of basketball."

6. Do men and women prefer different sports in your country?

"Men and women both like football. However men also like rugby which women think is too violent. Girls often like volleyball."

7. Can you tell me about any unusual sports in your country (culture)?

"Tibetans like horse racing. The 'short distance jogging' event is unusual because horses must have at least one leg touching the ground all the time, i.e. no jumping is permitted. The races are 3-5 km long."

Telephones 打电话

1. Do most people in your country (region) have telephones?

"Many people have telephones at home. People without telephones at home usually have them near their homes. Many people in the cities have mobile phones."

2. How often do you use telephones?

"I carry my mobile phone almost everywhere, but don't make or receive many calls. That's OK – I just carry in case I need it, for example if I'm going to a new bar and need directions. On the other hand, I send and receive many short messages. I rarely use my home phone."

3. Are mobile phones common in your country (region)?

"They are common in the cities, with young and middle-aged people. Almost everyone has one – students, taxi drivers, businessmen. Old people don't often have them."

4. For what reasons do people use mobile phones?

"People mainly use mobile phones to be able to contact other people at any time. Of course, they can be contacted at any time, too."

5. Are there places / situations where mobile phones shouldn't be used?

"Places or situations where you should switch your mobile phone off or not use it are: in an aircraft, in a class or lecture, during a religious gathering, during meetings, at the cinema, at a sports event, while driving, during a wedding ceremony."

6. What features can be found on mobile phones?

"The new Nokia is a stylish, compact mobile phone with several advanced features, including a camera and video recorder, with zoom capability. Of course, it has the more usual features, such as voice dialling, colour screen and games. It is a tri-band phone, so you can use it anywhere in the world. You can connect to the Internet, too."

Television (TV) 电视

1. How often do you watch TV?

"I watch TV between 10 and 12 hours a week. It depends a lot on my schedule and on the time of year. In summer, I watch less TV because I go out with friends. Sometimes, we watch TV at restaurants, but not friends' homes."

2. What kind of programmes do you watch?

"I like the historical dramas, folk music performances and military displays that are often on Chinese TV. Many people think they are boring, but I like them. My favourite programme is 'Professor Zhao Investigates'. It is shown every evening on Shanghai Television. The young professor hunts criminals in Shanghai. The stories take place in the 1920's."

3. Is watching TV a popular thing to do in your country?

"Yes. We can even watch TV at bars and restaurants. People want to know what is happening in the world. TV can tell us that easily. There are so many TV channels in China, but not all of them are national channels. People can easily find something they like to watch."

4. Do you often talk about TV programmes with friends?

"Not much. We normally talk about our work and families. We might talk about some issues that have been discussed on TV, but not the programmes."

5. Do you think that you watch too much TV?

"Yes and no. I watch about five hours a day. I like to relax and watch TV in the evenings. There are some very interesting programmes on. I always watch the news, because I am very interested in world events and what is happening in China. So, I do watch a lot of TV, but I know more about the world than most young Chinese people, so I don't really think I watch *too* much TV."

Transport 交通

1. How do you usually go to school / work?

"Because I live on campus I don't have far to go to my classrooms. I prefer to walk as I think this is better than using a bike. I can also chat to people on the way and I don't have to worry about my bicycle being stolen either!"

2. How good is the public transport system / network in your city / region?

"In my city, we only have buses, but the system is quite good. They are noisy and dirty, but there are many of them, so you don't need to wait long at the bus stop. The bus stops all have information in English, so foreign tourists can use the system, too."

3. If you go on a long journey, how do you prefer to travel?

"I prefer travelling by air. It is fast, but expensive. I earn enough money, so I can afford it. Travelling by train or by bus is not too expensive, but it takes too long."

4. Is transport expensive in your city / region / country?

"As I said, travelling by air is quite expensive, but other forms of transport are not. I think that using a car must be expensive. Buses in my city cost one RMB. Even travelling on the new, fast, luxury trains between Beijing and Hong Kong only costs about 1000 RMB."

5. Are traffic jams a problem where you live?

"Traffic jams are not a problem in my city, because the government has introduced laws to limit the number of cars on the streets. There are sometimes traffic jams if there is a car accident. People in other cities often complain about the traffic problems there. They should tell their local governments to take action."

Weather and Climate 天气与气候

1. What is your favourite time of the year?

"My favourite time of the year is winter. I love skiing near my hometown in Western Sichuan. Many people don't like the cold, but I don't mind. Of course, I have to wear warm clothes! The countryside looks very beautiful covered in snow. I will miss skiing when I go to England to study!"

2. Do you do different things in summer and in winter?

"No, I only study. Studying is very important, so I do it all year. If my room is cold in winter, I put on my jacket and study. I study indoors during the summer. It's too hot outside."

3. What do you do when the weather is wet?

"The wet weather doesn't change my schedule. I just keep studying. I like it when it rains in the summer, especially if there is a thunderstorm, because it makes the air cooler."

4. What kind of clothes do you wear in the spring / summer / autumn / winter?

"The summer is really hot where I live, so I wear as few clothes as possible. Many girls wear jeans even when the temperature is 40 degrees centigrade! I wear shorts or a skirt – much cooler! I also wear a blouse or T-shirt and sports shoes. In winter, it can be a little cold, so I wear a sweater and jeans. My favourite winter fashion colour is black, so I have many pairs of black jeans and a few black sweaters. In the summer, I wear much brighter colours – white, yellow, light blue and pink."

5. Is it often very hot / cold in your country / region / city?

"In Hainan, the temperature is usually between 17 and 33 degrees centigrade all year. So, it's not often very hot or very cold. There is about 1500 mm of rain each year, mainly between May and October. So, it can be quite wet. We sometimes have thunderstorms. It doesn't snow in Hainan!"

Weddings 婚礼

1. How do people usually celebrate weddings in your culture?

"There is a wedding ceremony, then a party. At the party, people make toasts and speeches. Sometimes the speeches are very long and boring. There's some music and dancing. Of course, there is a lot of food and drink."

2. Do people eat special food at weddings in your culture?

"I don't think that there is any special food that should be eaten. Perhaps noodles. I don't know. A friend told me that each table at a traditional Chinese wedding should have a whole duck, a whole chicken, eight cold dishes, and eight hot dishes. Eight is considered a lucky number. The number of guests at each table should also be eight."

3. What gifts do people usually buy for the bride and groom?

"In Britain, some couples make a scrapbook with pictures of the gifts they would like. People sign their names next to the pictures to indicate that they will buy that gift."

4. Do people wear special clothes at the wedding?

"The men wear suits and the ladies wear dresses. The bride sometimes wears a Chinese style dress, sometimes a Western one."

5. Do the bride and groom usually go on a honeymoon after the wedding?

"Yes, they do. The most popular places are big cities and the coast. They usually go for a month. Honeymoons are usually very expensive."

6. Which people are normally invited to a wedding?

"Close family, extended family, distant relatives, close friends, acquaintances, classmates, colleagues, bosses, and important local people."

7. What happens during the wedding ceremony?

"Western wedding ceremonies held in a church can last a long time, but not very much happens. The clergyman reads from the Bible, the couple make their wedding vows, then exchange rings and kiss. Many people choose to marry at a registry office. This ceremony has no religious aspect and is usually much smaller and shorter – and cheaper!"

Examiners have access to these model answers.
If you copy any of them, you could get a very low score in the IELTS test.

Your Country 你的国家

1. Is your country large?

"China has an area of about 9.6 (nine point six) million square kilometres. It is the third largest country in the world after Russia and Canada. It has a population of over 1.3 billion, the largest population of any country. China is about 40 times larger than Britain and has 20 times more people."

2. What is special or unique about your country?

"I think that the Terracotta Warriors are unique in the world. They were found by farmers in 1974 near the city of Xi'an in central China. Three pits have been discovered, with over 1000 warriors found so far. The site is easy to get to by bus from Xi'an and millions of people have visited it. The site is a UNESCO World Heritage Site."

3. Did / Do any world-famous people come from your country?

"Zu Chong Zhi lived from 429 to 500 A.D. He was a mathematician and astronomer, born in Jiankang (Nanjing). He came from a family of astronomers, so he learnt about it when he was young. His greatest achievement was the Daming Calendar, introduced in 465 A.D."

4. What industries are there in your country?

"There are many types of industry in China, such as light industry, heavy industry, the IT industry, the clothing industry, and the chemical industry. Heavy industry is mainly in the north-east of China. Car manufacturing is important in several large cities, such as Wuhan and Tianjin. The textile and food processing industries are common all over China. The IT industry is expanding quickly."

5. If you could change one thing about your country, what would it be?

"I would definitely stop the requirement for foreigners to have visas to come to China. This would certainly encourage more foreigners to come here to live, work, study and travel."

Your Home 你的家

1. Do you currently live in a flat / an apartment / a house / a dormitory?

"I live in a flat near the city centre. The flat is on the 12th floor in an old 24-floor building. It is only a ten-minute walk to my office. That's the main reason I like it. I live alone and it's a large flat for one person."

2. Could you describe your flat / apartment / house / dormitory?

"My flat is small – just a bedroom, living room, bathroom, and kitchen. The bedroom has a bed, a wardrobe, and a table and chair. It's small – about 15 square metres. The living room is a little bigger and has a sofa, two chairs, a table, and a TV. The kitchen and bathroom are simple and both very small."

3. What main items of furniture, or appliances, do you have in each room?

"There is a large, soft, black sofa in the living room, a big wardrobe made of wood in the bedroom. There is a microwave oven in the kitchen. I use it almost every day. Each room has air conditioning."

4. Is it a typical flat / apartment / house for people in your city?

"My apartment is much smaller than average. It's about 30 square metres. I don't need a big flat because I live alone. I think that the furniture – sofa, chairs, table, bed, wardrobe – is typical for a Chinese flat. Most of my friends have similar furniture in their flats."

5. Do you pay rent or does your home belong to you / your family?

"I rent the flat. It's a little expensive – 2000 RMB per month, but I'm happy with my flat and it's location. My friends pay less rent, but their flats are not in such good locations. In my city, rents are quite low. Most people pay about 1500 RMB per month for a flat like mine."

Your Hometown 你的家乡

1. Tell me something about your hometown.

"I come from Lhasa. It is famous for the Potola Palace, which is a World Heritage Site. It is in Tibet, a mountainous province in western China. Lhasa is 3760 metres above sea level. Now, Lhasa is developing quite quickly. Before, its development was slow because of its isolated location and high altitude."

2. What can a tourist see and do there?

"You can visit the markets and buy some things made by hand. The best is on Barhkor Street. Or you can visit the temples and monasteries. Jokhong Monastary and Drepung Temple are particularly famous. They are very quiet places."

3. Did / Do any famous people come from your hometown?

"The Lamas are the only famous people from my city. They are often born in the country-side and come to the city when they are very young. The Lamas are the spiritual leaders of the Tibetan people."

4. What industries are there in your hometown?

"The main industry is the tourist industry. Lhasa is not really suitable for large manufacturing industries, because of the climate and because it is isolated. At the moment, the construction industry employs many people. Roads are being reconstructed and a new railway to Golmud is being built. Many tourist sites, such as the Potola Palace, are being partly reconstructed after being damaged by bad weather and erosion."

5. If you could change one thing about your hometown, what would it be?

"I would improve the road and rail connections to other places. The government is already building a railway from Golmud to Lhasa, but I think there needs to be another line going to Sichuan. The problem is the mountainous land. The road connections are limited and often not good because of bad weather."

Your Job 你的工作

1. What do you do?

"I'm a refuse collector. Many people are surprised, because I have a university degree, but have such a basic job. I worked as an accountant for many years, but it was too stressful. I work almost every day. Some months I have the early shift, from 6 a.m. to 2 p.m. Other months, I get the late shift, from 2 p.m. to 10 p.m."

2. How long have you been doing this job?

"I have been doing this job for 5 years. I'd like to continue doing it for a few more years, but maybe not all my working life."

3. What exactly does your job involve?

"The job is quite simple. I go out with a team of refuse collectors and collect all the waste and litter that we see. Some people put their rubbish in plastic bags, which makes it easy to collect. Most people just leave it lying around on the ground, so we waste a lot of time cleaning it up. We have to be a little careful, because people may leave sharp items, such as broken glass, in the rubbish bags."

4. Tell me about your boss / colleagues.

"My colleagues are all very funny. I think you need a sense of humour to do this job. We often tell each other funny stories as we work. We get on with each other very well. Most of us are not very big, but one, 'Old Joe' is enormous. If people shout at us, Old Joe will just stare at them with a crazy smile on his face. They soon leave us alone. We wear uniforms, which are dirty after a few hours. That's OK – people expect us to look dirty!"

5. Are you satisfied with your job?

"I am very happy with my job, but I think we should get paid more. I know the work we do is very simple, but even a refuse collector has to have enough to live on."

Your Studies 你的学习

1. What do you study?

"I study genetics at Shi Du University, near Beijing. I'm doing a Ph.D. in Genetic Engineering. The faculty has 100 students and 10 professors. My courses include human genetics, plant genetics, and genetic modification."

2. Tell me something (more) about the school / university you attend.

"It's a small university about 50 kilometres from Beijing. The campus is very quiet, because it is not in a city and there are not so many students. The university is not very old. It's only 10 years old."

3. Tell me something (more) about your teachers / professors.

"I like my teachers. They explain things clearly and encourage you to develop your own ideas. The teacher-student relationship is very good and students and teachers can often be seen talking on campus or having a snack together."

4. What courses do you study?

"I am in the final year of my French degree. I study modules in modern French history, French literature, and French poetry. I have three two-hour classes on each module each week. Then I spend about ten hours a week reviewing and preparing for each module. My dissertation is on how the French are trying to limit the influence of English on the French language. I spend another ten hours a week on that."

5. How would you improve your courses / school?

"I would give the teachers money to do research. The results might interest the students. The students could help with the research, too. We also need more social facilities to use in the evenings. We could have a coffee bar for example. Apart from those things, I'm very satisfied with the school."

Student's Notes:

Part Two Topics

口试第二阶段常见话题

An Achievement 一次成功

Tell me about a great achievement your country has made.
You should say: what the achievement is (was)
why it is (was) a great achievement
how it was accomplished and over what period
and explain how most people in your country view this achievement today.

"One of the great achievements that China has made is winning the bid to hold the Olympic games in 2008. I still remember the evening in Ningbo when it was announced on TV that we had won. All the students went mad and cheered and held celebrations. Of course it was not easy for China to win the bid. Perhaps the greatest obstacle was air pollution in Beijing. The government is trying its best to reduce it by moving a lot of factories from the city centre to the outskirts and by limiting the use of coal and charcoal burners. There is a lot of development going on now in Beijing as new stadiums are built and roads are widened. The subway is being extended too. These will remain in place long after the Olympics are over, so will benefit the locals. The learning of English has taken on a new meaning as this will be the language used to communicate with the many tourists who will come for the Games. Even police officers are learning it."

An Advertisement 一则广告

Tell me about an advertisement.
You should say: what product or service is advertised
what the advertisement shows or showed
why you remember this advertisement in particular
and say whether you think the advertisement is/was effective.

"In Britain, there was a memorable television advertisement for a chocolate snack. A photographer set up his camera on a tripod in front of the panda cage at a zoo. Pandas are notoriously shy and so the man expected a long wait before the panda came out and gave him the chance to take a photograph. The man waited patiently behind his camera. Phrases at the bottom of the screen such as '2 hours later ...' told you that the man had been waiting for a long time. Eventually, the man decided to take a break and turned around to sit down and eat the chocolate snack being advertised. When he did so, the panda came out and danced and roller-skated around the cage, making faces at the man. The man was sitting with his back to the cage, so he couldn't see the panda doing this. As the man finished his snack and resumed his wait behind his camera, the cheeky panda hid once more. And so the man continued waiting for his chance to take a photograph ..."

An Ambition 一个愿望

Tell me about an ambition you have in life.

You should say: what the ambition is
whether you really believe you will ever achieve it
what you must do in order to achieve it
and whether you will need any help.

"My ambition in life is to marry and have children. Now this is a fairly normal ambition which most people have but it is one that I find difficult to achieve. Most women find me handsome and intelligent so there is never a shortage of applicants. My trouble is that I am a bit of a perfectionist and my dream girl would be tall, pretty, clever, kind and caring. I find that many girls I meet have some of these characteristics but not all of them. Now I am sure that there are plenty of such girls in Beijing but how do I meet them? I don't go to bars much so the only way to meet girls is on the Internet. So far I have met quite a few but they all fall short in some way. Perhaps I should arrange to meet a matchmaker and tell him my requirements and then sit back and await developments. But I really need to take some action soon as I am growing older day by day and if I want to have children then it is better while I am still young."

An Animal 一种动物

Tell me about an animal.

You should say: what the animal is and where it lives
what the animal looks like and how it behaves
how this animal is special
and explain why you chose to talk about this animal.

"The lion is known as the king of the jungle and rightly so for it has few natural enemies. It is found mainly in Africa and is the largest member of the cat family. It is four-legged with a long tail. The male has a large mane of hair whilst the female does not. One unusual aspect of the lion's anatomy is that as the male lion gets older its head gets bigger. Lions live together in a group called a pride which hunts together. They are carnivorous and kill only for food. Sometimes it will kill people but this is rare as most lions are afraid of man. Many attempts have been made to domesticate this wild animal but all have failed so far. What I like about the lion is the sense of majesty it displays as it prowls its territory. It is afraid of no other animal and roars to announce its presence and intimidate other animals."

An Artistic Skill 一种艺术技巧

Tell me about an artistic skill you wish you had or wish you could learn.

You should say: what the skill is and where you could learn it
why you would like to have or learn it
how it might change you or your life
and explain how you would use your new skill.

"I would love to be able to play the piano. I have no musical ability at all and cannot sing well either but I really envy those who can. To be able to sit down at a piano and produce notes and melodies that are instantly recognisable and pleasing to the ear is my dream. I don't want to be a concert pianist but just good enough to play well-known songs. I think that playing a musical instrument is a really useful ability, as it not only brings pleasure to yourself, but other people too. It would be nice to be present at a party where there was a piano in the room and provide music and fun for all the guests. I suppose that I would have to find someone who could teach me and I know that perhaps it would take a long time and be really hard work, but I think it would be worth it. Not only would I be able to play music but I could learn the stories about the songs and their composers."

Bad Habits 坏习惯

Tell me about one or two bad habits you have.

You should say: what the bad habits are and how long you have had it/them
why these habits are bad and what you can do about them
whether other people also have this/these bad habits
and say whether you think having bad habits is really *so* bad.

"A bad habit I have is smoking. I first started smoking at school during breaks when I would light up in the toilets. Gradually I started smoking more and more until I was smoking about 30 a day. When I was in my early thirties I stopped smoking but recently I have started again and chain-smoking heavily. I would like to stop as a lot of my friends don't like me smoking, especially my boyfriend. I know it is a bad habit because it is not doing my health any good. I find I cough more and am frequently out of breath. The smoke gets everywhere and my clothes constantly smell of tobacco. I wish I could give up but don't seem to have the necessary willpower or motivation at the moment. Sometimes I really like to smoke but most of the time I don't. I find that my body wants nicotine and I cannot resist. I know a lot of people in China smoke and it is a bad habit and maybe one day I will stop again."

A Book 一本书

Tell me about a book you have read.

You should say: which book it was and when you read it
what feelings you had whilst reading it
if you have read other books by the same author
and how it influenced you, if at all.

"I have always liked reading so books are never far away from me. One of the most recent books that I have read is 'The Merchant of Venice' by William Shakespeare. This is a classic of English literature but difficult to read in the original form. Words have changed their meaning and so a glossary is an essential accessory. This is a book that needs to be read slowly and carefully, sipped like a delicate wine. The story is a simple one of love and greed with a courtroom battle fit to rival the best of Grisham. On to the stage steps the menacing, leering figure of Shylock – the mercenary moneylender who demands his pound of flesh. Against him stands Portia, dressed as a male lawyer who defends her lover. Good overcomes evil and Portia wins her case and the two lovers live happily ever after. Many quotations have come into popular use in the English language from this book including 'the quality of mercy is not strained'."

A Ceremonial Event 一次庆典活动

Tell me about a ceremonial event that you either watched or attended.

You should say: what the event was and where it took place
if it is a regular event or a 'one-off'
how you felt about it
and explain why you think it is special.

"When I completed my master's degree I was looking forward to the graduation ceremony because I missed the one for my bachelor's degree as I was in Taiwan at the time. Of course I went to it mainly because of my parents. They had supported me during my education and this was a great opportunity for them to see the results of my hard work. The ceremony was held in an old civic building in the heart of the town. I had rented my gown and mortar board earlier that day and enjoyed walking through the streets enjoying the attention I received from curious passers-by. Sitting in the hall I waited nervously for my name to be called. When it was I made my way up to the podium, accepted my degree, waited for my mother to take a photo, and then proudly returned to my seat and sat down. Afterwards we had tea on the college lawn and took several photos. What a memorable day it was!"

A Change in Your Life 生活中的一次变化

Tell me about a great change that occurred at some point in your life.

You should say: what the change was and when it happened
if it was special for you or is usual for other people too
how it has changed your life
and explain your feelings about it.

"One of the greatest changes that happened in my life was when I was in my early forties. I was working in an accountant's office but found the work boring and repetitive. So I decided to change my career and life by going to university. I had not gone to university when I left school as most other students did. I wanted to be a teacher so I chose my major and spent a year going to evening classes in order to get the required university entrance grades. I chose several universities and visited most of them. Finally I decided to choose Lhasa in Tibet, which was far away from my home, partly because I wanted a change of scenery. I sold my house and bought a large car into which I put all my belongings and drove to my new home. I soon made friends among my classmates and the three years passed quickly. At last, the time came when I proudly held my bachelor's degree in my hand and began a new career in teaching."

A City 一座城市

Tell me about a city you have visited.

You should say: where the city is and when you went there
what people can see and do in that city
why that city is special
and explain why your visit to that city was memorable.

"One of the nicest cities I have ever visited is the small ancient city of Cambridge. As everyone knows, Cambridge is famous for its university. Founded nearly 800 years ago the university dominates the city with its medieval and gothic-style colleges and buildings. There are 31 colleges and entrance to most of them is free. Conducted tours are available but you don't have time to visit all of them. When night falls and you wander around these ancient alleys and courtyards you could almost imagine that you were transported back into the time of the Tudors. Step away from the quiet of the quads and suddenly Cambridge is turned into a lively, bustling city full of noisy students riding their bikes to college or library. Running through the centre of the city is the river Cam. You cannot visit Cambridge without seeing this river and then taking a ride on one of the many punts that are for hire. Your guide will tell you many interesting stories as you pass college after college on your way downstream past ducks, picnickers and the odd studious student."

Examiners have access to these model answers.
If you copy any of them, you could get a very low score in the IELTS test.

A Classmate 一名同学

Tell me about one of your classmates.

You should say: who the classmate is/was and how you met them
what the classmate is/was like
whether you had a good relationship
and say whether other people in your class have/had a similar opinion of this person.

"In university one of my classmates was an older student in his thirties. He was married with a little girl and his name was Chris. He was about the same height as me but a little heavier in weight. Most of the students were Northern Irish but we both came from England and this helped to form a bond between us. We tended to study together in the library and often had our meals together. Sometimes I would go to his house for a meal or a cup of coffee and a chat. I found that he was easy to get along with and full of good advice and suggestions when it came to dealing with problems in my life. Other students held the same opinion about him and in our final year he was elected student chairman. Even though we have both left university and pursued different careers we still keep in touch regularly by email."

A Controversial Issue 一个有争议的话题

Tell me about a controversial issue in your country.

You should say: what the issue is and why it is so controversial
what the arguments are on this issue
what most people think about it
and explain what your opinion on this issue is.

"The use of SMS messages to send advertisements is a hot issue – though less controversial as the number of people who don't mind them or welcome them is relatively small. The real issue seems to be how to deal with it. Controls could lead people to believe that the government is policing their communications. No controls mean that people could be annoyed by the number of advertising messages they receive. They could also be tricked by disreputable businessmen. It is controversial because many business people do not see the problem with advertising in this way. One way of solving this problem has been suggested. That way is to make a database of people who do not wish to receive SMS advertisements. Any company then sending advertisements to people on the list would face a penalty. I think this is a great idea."

A Cultural Event 一次文化活动

Tell me about a cultural event that you either saw on TV or went to.

You should say: what the event was and where it took place
if it is a national event or only local / regional
if it attracted a wide range of people
and how you felt about it.

"During Spring Festival I went with a friend to an old renowned teahouse in the centre of Beijing. We paid our entrance fee, sat near the stage, drank our tea and ate different kinds of sweets. As the time of the performance approached, the tables began to fill up, mainly with Chinese, but with some foreigners too. Finally the curtain rose and onstage came a splendidly dressed middle-aged lady who introduced the acts. There were several musical groups, some dancing girls, a comedy duo, a lady who sang opera and a short play but for me the highlight of the evening was a short fat bald man. This unlikely star of the night carried a small earthenware pot which he balanced on his head and then proceeded to tip and turn and swivel it every which way. As if this was not enough he exchanged the small pot for another which was almost as big as he was. Again he did exactly the same with the large pot as he had done previously with the small one. Quite rightly, he received the loudest applause of the evening."

An Economic Activity 一次经济活动

Tell me about an important economic activity in your country.

You should say: what the activity is and where it takes place
how it is important in your life
how it has developed over the last 20 years
and explain why it is important to your country.

"China is the world's biggest market for tobacco. It has 300 million smokers who mainly smoke local brands. So cigarette production is a major economic activity in China and especially in Yunnan which is considered to be the home of the best Chinese tobacco. It has the largest tobacco leaf growing area in the world but is facing demands to improve its production and curing. There are also increasing problems with counterfeit cigarettes which can be produced more cheaply and which evade the government tax. As the cigarette tax provides 10% of its income the Chinese government is rightly worried. Despite a restricted market and a ban on advertising, this is an industry that just grows and grows. 46% of college students admit to being smokers. As most of the people who smoke are male there is obvious enormous potential among females. As a smoker myself I rarely see a girl who smokes and this is because it is considered to be socially taboo in China for a woman to smoke. Despite this (or perhaps because of this!) there is a growing number of women who smoke."

Examiners have access to these model answers.
If you copy any of them, you could get a very low score in the IELTS test.

An Economic Issue 一个经济问题

Tell me about an economic issue that is facing your country.

You should say: what the issue is and why it is important
how it affects you personally
how the government is treating this issue
and explain how this issue may develop in the future.

"One major economic issue that is facing China is the increasing gap between the rich and the poor, the eastern part of China and the western part. Most of China's wealthiest people live in a narrow strip along its Eastern coast. This is where its major cities like Beijing and Shanghai lie. Its economic advantages are that it is an area from which it is easy to conduct trade with other countries. To the west are the poorer regions where most farmers have to live on subsistence earnings. The roads and communications are poor and this adds to the cost of transporting any goods. Living standards are poor, as is health and education. The government has reacted to this widening gulf by cutting the taxes farmers pay and by encouraging graduates to live and work there. It is seeking to invest capital in these poorer regions to raise the overall economic level."

The Education System 教育体制

Tell me about the education system in your country.

You should say: at what ages students go to different schools
what the advantages and disadvantages of the system are
how the system is changing
and explain what changes you would like to see.

"In Britain we have a three tier educational system. Firstly there is primary education for pupils aged 5 to 11. Next there is secondary education for pupils aged 11 to 16 or 18 and then there is tertiary or university education. In primary education there used to be what was known as the 11 plus exam where pupils were streamed by ability into either grammar schools (if you passed the exam) or into secondary schools if you failed. Now this has been done away with and all secondary education is at the same level. Pupils can either leave secondary education at age 16 or stay on for a further two years to take 'A' levels which are necessary for university entrance. Universities are open to entrants regardless of age and indeed a quarter are considered mature students – that is over the age of 21. It is very common to find computers at all levels in schools now and the majority of school leavers are computer literate."

Examiners have access to these model answers.
If you copy any of them, you could get a very low score in the IELTS test.

An Environmental Problem 一个环境问题

Tell me about an environmental problem that is facing your country.

You should say:
- what the problem is
- how it arose
- how it influences life in your country
- and explain how this problem could be solved.

"Although living in Beijing has its advantages such as access to some of the most important cultural sites in China there is a downside. Every spring when the weather is cool and refreshing and heralds the arrival of flowers and green leaves and trees there also arrives an unwelcome visitor – sandstorms. These dust storms originate in the Gobi desert and are brought by winds to Beijing. When this happens the sand gets everywhere, clogging up noses and stinging the eyes and making it difficult to see or breathe. Residents of Beijing prefer to stay indoors at these times and rarely venture outside. The sand gets everywhere, entering your home through gaps in the doors and windows. Everything gets covered with sand making things dirty, unpleasant and smelly. To overcome this problem the government has planted acres of trees as a windbreak and sand catcher to stop the sand reaching the capital."

An Ethnic Minority 一个少数民族

Tell me about an ethnic minority in your country.

You should say:
- what the minority is called and where the people live
- how the people there are special or different to other ethnic groups in your country
- what traditions or festivals they have
- and say whether you would like to live with this ethnic minority.

"The Mosuo are a minority that live in north-west Yunnan. The Mosuo are known for their matriarchal society. Women are the heads of families and husband-wife relationships do not exist. Fathers usually maintain few links with their children. Mainly, they look after their sisters' children. Now their privacy and way of life are being threatened by the arrival of thousands of tourists. On the other hand, this tourism has increased the wealth of the community."

A Famous Person 一个著名的人物

Tell me about a famous person who you particularly admire.

You should say: who the person is (was) and why they are (were) famous
why you particularly admire them
how they contribute(d) to society
and say what questions you would ask this person if you met them.

"My major is Genetics and in this field, the person I admired most, is Mendel who is known as the father of Genetics. He was an Austrian scientist who was the first to discover the law of Genetics. He did a number of experiments on inheritance in pea plants. However, it turns out that the rules which Mendel deduced from studies of peas are equally applicable to human inheritance and it is convenient to follow his train of logic beginning with characteristics determined by a single gene and moving on to the complications introduced by multiple genes. He did not know about genes and chromosomes: what he called 'factors' we now call genes. Mendel also did not know about cell division as he had not seen diagrams or slides of mitosis and meiosis. Mendel was not a famous scholar at that time and so people thought of him as a missionary rather than a scientist. So his opinions and some scientific findings that he published did not attract people's notice and were buried for 34 long years! Of course, I want to be a person like Mendel, and I will work hard to make some great discovery in the biology field. I'm looking forward to the coming of that day."

A Film 一部电影

Tell me about a film you have seen.

You should say: what the title of the film was and where you saw it
what the story (plot) involves
whether you have seen other films by the same director
and explain how you feel about this film.

"Today my friends advised me that I should see a movie called "Outbreak" to get a true feeling about terrible infectious diseases. The star of this movie is called Dustin Hoffman who is a previous Oscar winner. In this movie the American Health Department have discovered a new kind of bacteria which causes people to die within a few hours. It is let loose in a small village in Africa where Hoffman is the local doctor. Hoffman is amazed and then frightened as so many of the villagers die within such a small time. The Health Department have an antidote but instead of using it to destroy the bacteria the Department aims to use the deadly virus as a biological weapon. Unfortunately the virus mutates from a blood-borne virus to an air-borne one and deaths multiply. Hoffman comes to the rescue, steals the antidote and saves the people. My friends said that after they saw the movie they became even more scared about SARS."

A Form of Transport 一种交通方式

Tell me about a form of transport that you enjoy using.

You should say:
- what the form of transport is and how often you use it
- its advantages and disadvantages
- how much other people use it and why
- and explain why you enjoy using it so much.

"Of all the forms of transport that are available to man the one I like the best is the bicycle. It is easy to use, convenient to leave outside your destination and easy to mend if it breaks. It is one of the cheapest methods of travel and available to all. The bicycle is very easy to learn how to ride, as every child knows, and once mastered is never forgotten. In these days of traffic congestion, the bicycle is easy to manoeuvre and, more importantly, easy to park. The bicycle can be chained and left unattended just about anywhere. Most important is the feeling when you ride your machine. The cool breeze against your face, the landscape sliding past and the freedom to travel anywhere and everywhere whenever you like. This mobility and independence of travel means that it is easy to organise an outing or a picnic to a local beauty spot with some friends."

A Friend 一个朋友

Tell me about one of your friends.

You should say:
- who the friend is and how you first met him / her
- what you enjoy doing together
- what he / she is like and looks like
- and explain why your friendship is so special.

"My closest friend is called Google. He used to be one of my PhD students in Beida in my English speaking class. One day he invited me to his dorm to have a meal with him. His girlfriend was also there and we spent a very enjoyable evening together. Since then we have met many times - in his office, at a restaurant, at my home, and on the campus. We normally like to have a meal together and catch up on each other's news. He is average height for a Chinese and of slim build. He wears glasses and usually has a wide grin on his face. It is perhaps his lively sense of humour that attracts me the most. That and the fact that we can talk about anything, and usually do, is another plus factor in his favour. As a friend he is always willing to make time for me and help me with any problems I might have. Why is he interested in me? He is studying psychology and so he probably finds me an interesting case study!"

A Game 一种游戏

Tell me about a game that you have played.

You should say: what the game was and what you need to play
if it is widely played in your country
how it is played
and say why you think it is a good way to spend time.

"When I was at school I used to enjoy playing rugby. We didn't play football as this was not a sport played at my school. Rugby is an English game played with a team of 15 players and the ball is oval shaped. Unlike football, in rugby the ball can be handled as well as kicked. It is a very physical sport because tackling is allowed. The aim is to score tries by touching down the ball at the opposite end of the pitch. Once a try is scored then the ball can be kicked between the goal posts to score more points. Because I could run very fast I played on the wing and I really enjoyed catching the ball and trying to score a try. But because I am very short-sighted and couldn't play wearing my glasses I sometimes missed the ball or would drop it. So I moved position and became a forward. Actually I liked this better because it meant that I was involved in the game more. Rugby helped to keep me fit and also made me stronger. Then I could play two games in a day but now I only watch rugby on TV."

A Historical Event 一个历史事件

Tell me about a historical event.

You should say: what the event was and when and where it took place
which famous people were involved in this event
why this event was important
and explain why you find this event interesting.

"Every English schoolboy knows that 1066 stands for the battle of Hastings – the last time England was successfully invaded and conquered by a foreign army. It all started when Edward the Confessor, King of England, died childless. There were two rivals for the throne, firstly, Harold Godwinson, grandson of a Viking warrior and son of Earl Godwin, father-in-law of the late king. Secondly, there was Duke William of Normandy who was the grand-nephew of Edward the Confessor's mother. Harold was crowned king by the English nobles but then had to contend with a rebellion by his brother in the north. William invaded England on the south coast at Hastings. Harold, having defeated his brother, raced south. Harold arranged his forces on a hill forcing William to attack uphill. But William used archers and cavalry to great effect and Harold was wounded in the eye by a Norman arrow. He died and this demoralised his men so that they were easily defeated by the Norman invaders."

Examiners have access to these model answers.
If you copy any of them, you could get a very low score in the IELTS test.

A Hobby or Interest 一种爱好或兴趣

Tell me about a hobby or an interest that you have.

You should say: what the hobby or interest is
when and why you took up this hobby or interest
whether you expect to continue with this hobby or interest
and explain how this hobby or interest affects the other aspects of your life.

"My interests and hobbies are very broad and extensive. And with the rise of age, my interests and hobbies have become more and more active, although sometimes I am quiet and introverted. I have a preference for outdoors sports such as going hiking, flying kites, playing badminton and so on. For one thing, I am very keen on flying kites. In fact, kite flying is both fun and creative not only for children but also for adults. A bright shining sun, a blue sky, and a gentle breeze make the most favourable weather for flying a kite. As a child, I enjoyed flying a kite in a very simple way, but now I have learned some ways of manipulating it in different wind conditions. When the wind blows really hard, I am faced with more challenges to my kite-flying skill, which is what I like. What's more, I can even make a kite myself. I can make whatever shape or form I prefer, such as a butterfly or a dragon."

A Holiday 一个假日

Tell me about a holiday you have taken.

You should say: when and where you went on the holiday
if it is a popular holiday destination
what you did on the holiday
and what was special about it.

"During the Spring Festival I had several weeks holiday so I decided to go to a place I had always wanted to visit – Yunnan. Several of my students come from that province and recommended it, so I booked the flights and hotels with my tour agency, packed my bags and off I went. I arrived in Kunming, which is the capital of Yunnan, settled into my hotel and then organised some local trips. There was a visit to the site of the World Expo held a few years ago where I could see different kinds of trees, plants and flowers. I particularly enjoyed visiting an evening gala where there were several performances. A buffet was provided and you could help yourself to as much food or drink as you wanted. I visited an elephant camp and watched them as they went through their routines. They washed themselves in a stream and then played football, with one of the elephants acting as goalkeeper and another taking penalty kicks. I would certainly go again."

Examiners have access to these model answers.
If you copy any of them, you could get a very low score in the IELTS test.

A Hotel 一家旅馆

Tell me about a hotel.

You should say: where the hotel is and what it is called
what the hotel looks like
what facilities the hotel has
and say whether you often stay in hotels.

"The Burj Al-Arab hotel in the United Arab Emirates, is widely considered to be the best hotel in the world. It has a distinctive shape — like a sail. It is 321 metres high, and stands on a man-made island, 280 metres from the shore of Jumeirah Beach, just outside Dubai. The hotel has 202 suites, including 2 Presidential Suites and 2 Royal Suites. The hotel has 7 restaurants, serving Arab, European, and International dishes. There is live music all day. As you would expect from such a wonderful hotel, there is a spa and a fully equipped fitness centre. The hotel has three swimming pools, including one specially designed for families. Near the hotel, there are tennis courts, golf courses, and beaches. They are all lit at night, so you can enjoy yourself 24 hours a day, if you have the energy! Of course, being right by the sea, you can also enjoy several water sports such as sailing, water skiing, and windsurfing, or go scuba diving!"

An Important Structure 一座重要建筑物

Tell me about an important structure in your city or country.

You should say: what the structure is and what it is used for
what the structure is made of and what it looks like
how it has changed the area around it
and say what you thought of the structure the first time you saw it.

"Big Ben is one of London's best-known landmarks, and looks most spectacular at night when the clock faces are illuminated. Most people think that Big Ben is the name of the clock but the name Big Ben actually refers not to the clock or the clock-tower itself, but to the 13 ton bell hung within which was cast in 1858 at the Whitechapel Bell Foundry in East London. To this day one of the largest bells they have ever cast. The bell was named after the first commissioner of works, Sir Benjamin Hall. Each of the four clock faces is over 7m in diameter. When Parliament sits by night a light in the Clock Tower burns above Big Ben. Old pennies act as counterweights to ensure Big Ben keeps time to the nearest second. There are even cells within the clock tower where Members of Parliament can be imprisoned for a breach of parliamentary privilege, though this is rare; the last recorded case was in 1880."

A Job 一种工作

Tell me about a job that you have never had, but would like to have.

You should say: what the job is and why you want to do it
if it requires any special skills or abilities
how it would change your personal life
and explain how you might get this job in the future.

"A job I would really like to have is that of holiday writer. I would love to be able to travel to distant and exotic places and then write about these places so that people choosing a holiday destination might pick the one that I had written about. Of course I would need to be able to write well and objectively so that my readers would be able to see what I had seen and then decide for themselves if this would be a good place for them to visit. One of the exciting things about being a holiday writer is having several free holidays a year and staying in nice comfortable hotels. It would be nice to be able to choose which countries and cities to visit but perhaps that may not be possible. To go skiing in the Alps in midwinter or sunbathing in the Caribbean would make a nice change from dry, dusty Beijing! But it is not all holiday as I would have to visit many places and take notes and then spend evenings writing about what I have experienced. And then the magazine has to approve the work and when it is published I would have to wait for my pay!"

Learning English 学英语

Tell me about your experience of learning English.

You should say: when you started learning English and why
how you have learnt English and with which people
how it has changed your life so far
and say why you think it will be useful to you in the future.

"I have been learning English for over 10 years now but still have great difficulty in speaking it. We start learning English in primary school. The education system here in China emphasises the importance of exams and so we merely learn English in order to pass them. I know that English is a global language and that if I want to work for an international company then it is necessary to be able to speak it. But my spoken English is so poor that I am not confident to use it. I must admit that I rarely use English outside of class because I just don't come into contact with foreigners. Even if I did I would be too shy to speak. I never had a foreign teacher at school and so am not used to speaking with them. My reading and writing skills are OK but my listening is poor. Whenever I watch a Hollywood movie I always listen to it in Chinese because the actors speak too fast for me to follow them. I try to read English magazines like College Times because it is always full of interesting articles and really helps me to improve my English."

Making Yourself a Better Person 完善自己

Tell me about how you could make yourself a better person.

You should say: what the change or improvement would be
why you have not made the change or improvement yet
if you would need the help of other people
and explain how your life would be better as a result.

"As human beings are composed of at least three parts, physical, mental and spiritual, then if I want to make myself a better person I need to improve each of these areas. Although not fat, I could do with exercising. At the moment the only exercise I do is walking to and from work. And work is only ten minutes away! Perhaps I could take up a sport or join a fitness club. I could also improve my appearance by going shopping for some new clothes. A new wardrobe would do wonders! I once read that if you have regular mental challenges then this can prolong your life. Reading something other than novels would certainly help, as would playing chess or even Mah Jong. I could always learn a new skill such as a language or go to evening class. As I have a spiritual side I could, for example, go to church every week or learn meditation and yoga. An awareness of a spiritual being who could help through life's crisis has been of enormous help to friends I know and they have often told me of answers to prayer."

A Meal 一顿饭

Tell me about a meal that you either cooked or ate.

You should say: what the meal consisted of and who made it
if it was for a special occasion
where you cooked it or ate it
and explain why the meal was so special.

"I am not a cook and can only boil eggs but I do appreciate good food and a good meal is one that should be enjoyed and remembered. One of the best meals I ever had was when I was invited by one of the Chinese teachers at the university where I taught English to his home for a meal. He had just moved into a new flat and so this was a great opportunity to visit him. He prepared all the dishes himself and while waiting for the meal to be cooked we drank some local beer as well as some strong Chinese wine. The food was simple with several different courses. We ate at a small table until we were full and drank to our hearts content. What was memorable about the meal was not the food or drink but the company. My host had many amusing stories to tell and the time passed quickly. It was my first introduction into a Chinese home and to be treated not just as a guest but as a friend made this meal so special for me."

A Memorable Experience 一次难忘的经历

Tell me about a memorable experience you have had.

You should say: what the experience was
if you experienced it alone or with other people
where and when the experience took place
and explain how it has influenced you afterwards.

"During my three years in college, I established a speech group with several other students sponsored by some companies to go to the countryside and towns to impart this message and help those in need. Once we went to one of the poorest towns in Henan province. The local government organized 2,000 students to come to our speech. It was a severe winter with no heat in the auditorium, but I saw those students sitting quietly, listening so attentively, taking their notes once in a while. Their eyes were shining, eager to learn and to grow. I found myself shivering, yet my heart was hot. I told them of my origin, my ups and downs, my dreams and my beliefs. I hoped when they stepped out of this auditorium, some of them would be bold enough to pursue their dreams, to follow their heart and get new lives. At the end of the speech, I sang a song to them while I saw tears rolling down some of the faces. That was one of the most unforgettable moments of my life."

Parents 父母亲

Tell me about your parents.

You should say: what they do at work and in their free time
something about their characters
how they are similar and how they are different
and say how similar to your parents you think you are.

"My father was a middle school teacher of politics but now works as a quality control inspector. My mother was a nurse but retired a year ago. She is quite slim because she did a lot of walking in her job and she likes to climb mountains at the weekend. My father though, is a little fat, partly because he doesn't take any exercise. He is strict with me and often tells me off whereas my mother is more patient and understanding. Perhaps this is because she is a mother and a nurse. I have learned many valuable lessons from them, especially the value of hard work and the importance of being honest and trustworthy. Sometimes, when I was growing up, I felt a little lonely because I am an only child but my parents have always shown their love towards me and never spoiled me, which is what happens in some one child families. I have some of my father's qualities and also some of my mother's. When I get married I hope I can be as good a parent as they have been to me."

A Party 一次聚会

Tell me about a party you have been to.

You should say: where the party was held and who went
what the party was like
what happened at the party
and say whether you often go to parties.

"Parties are common in China for students and I have been invited to many. One party was held by my English class. They took over a small restaurant on campus and prepared and cooked the food themselves. We all ate and drank till we could eat and drink no more and then the fun started. We moved to a large room and sat at tables around the dance floor. At each table there would be bottles of water and some fruit. Several performances were planned by the class and, as is normal in China, a boy and a girl introduced each act. Of course there were songs sung and some dancers. As there were some English teachers present we were asked to do a performance each."

A Person Who Has Influenced You 一个对你有影响的人

Tell me about a person who has greatly influenced you.

You should say: who the person is (was)
how you came into contact with this person
how they have influenced you and why
and whether this person has also influenced other people.

"Obviously our parents influence us the most and this is certainly true with me. My parents divorced when I was about 3 and my mother remarried when I was 15. My new stepfather was a local businessman and active in politics. He had a large house out in the countryside filled with new and old furniture. His greatest love was art and especially modern art. I came to love the paintings in the house and often went with him to museums and art galleries. Eventually I started to collect paintings too. At first the paintings I collected were similar in style to my stepfather's but gradually I developed in a different way. I preferred to collect the work of newer, unknown artists and soon built up a large collection. My stepfather liked to hold dinner parties or go out to restaurants and so I also learned to appreciate good food and wine."

A Person You Would Like to Spend a Day with 你想共度一日的人

Tell me about a person you would like to spend a day with.

You should say: who the person is
what you would do together
what questions you would ask this person
and explain why you would choose to spend a day with them in particular.

"Perhaps the person I would love to spend a day with is Jesus. Of all the historical figures who has ever lived he is perhaps the most interesting. Not every one can claim that he is the Son of God! If we were to have a meal together perhaps he would change water into wine just like he did at Cana. Perhaps a woman would come up to him and fall at his feet and kiss them like Mary Magdalene did once. After lunch we could take a stroll around the city and maybe crowds would follow him waiting for him to speak just as they followed him around Galilee. He was admired as the greatest teacher who ever lived, a man who could answer the most difficult questions with ease, so I could ask him whatever I wanted. He was also a healer so maybe he could cure my short-sightedness! Perhaps the reason why I would like to meet him is a simple one. I would love to know what he looked like. No pictures exist of him and there are no descriptions of him recorded by his disciples in the New Testament."

A Piece of Music or a Song 一首音乐或一首歌

Tell me about a piece of music or a song that you particularly enjoy.

You should say: what the music/song is and where/when you first heard it
who wrote it or sings it
if it is popular with other people
and explain your feelings when you hear this music or song.

"Someone once said that 'Music soothes the savage breast' and certainly I enjoy listening to music, in particular the works of the Beatles. They were the first superband, also known as the 'Fab Four,' and they influenced my early formative years not only as far as my music was concerned but my dress too and the length of my hair. Their music ranged from rock and roll to sentimental love songs and I loved them all. In particular I loved the album 'Rubber Soul' best of all. This album, which is in the top ten favourite albums of all time, contains the song 'Norwegian Wood'. I could never really understand the song but I liked the lyrics and the music. I used to sing it or hum it wherever I went. It is sung by John Lennon in his distinctive nasal whine and tells the story of a girl who invited him to stay the night. He does so and sleeps in the bath which I thought was weird but I still liked it anyway."

A Piece of News 一则新闻

Tell me about a piece of news you heard or read recently.

You should say: what the news was and where you heard or read it
if it was significant for many people
how it has changed, or will change, people's lives
and explain how you felt when you heard or read this news.

"I read a story recently about a Scandinavian couple who lived by the sea. One day the wife was walking along the beach when she lost an earring. It fell into the sea and despite her best efforts she could not find it. A week later her husband, a keen fisherman, caught a fish near where his wife had lost the earring. He took it home and his wife prepared it for their dinner. Imagine her surprise and amazement when she cut it open and emptied its stomach to find her earring. The couple could not believe that such an amazing circumstance could happen to them. I suppose all of us could tell of lesser coincidences when we are thinking of a person and then happen to meet them in the street or we bump into someone who happens to come from the same hometown as we do. This raises the question of why such coincidences happen and whether they happen more frequently than we believe."

A Place You Have Visited 一个你参观过的地方

Tell me about a place you have visited.

You should say: where the place is and why you went there
if it is a popular place for people to go to
how it has changed or may change
and explain how you felt when you went there for the first time.

"One of the most popular places to visit in Beijing is the Summer Palace and for me it has the distinct advantage of being near where I work! It used to be the summer residence of the emperors and is built on a grand scale, especially the gardens and lakes. The lake is modelled on the famous West Lake of Hangzhou and this is the part I like best. Once I walked the entire circumference of the lake but normally I just like to find a quiet spot and relax and enjoy the scenery. Sometimes I like to take a boat to one of the islands and then explore it. The Long Pavilion is quite famous but easily gets crowded. Once I was walking along it and got accosted by a young man who invited me into his shop. He was selling paintings but I did not like any of them so soon left. The Summer Palace is a wonderful place to visit and you can have many enjoyable hours there but it is best not to visit it during holiday times or at weekends as it gets very crowded then."

A Place You Would Like to Visit
一个你想去参观的地方

Tell me about a place you would like to visit.
You should say: where the place is and what you would do there
if you know anyone who has already been there
how you first heard of this place
and explain why you would like to go there so much.

"I would love to visit Tibet. Now that I am in China it would be very easy to arrange a tour of this wonderful and remote country. I have heard a lot about Tibet. The high mountains and monasteries perched on them would be amazing to see. Tibet is the home of the Himalayas, which includes Mount Everest, the highest mountain in the world. I know that there are some difficulties in visiting Tibet such as visa problems but these can be overcome by travelling in a group. Perhaps the biggest problem is the high altitude, which can cause breathing difficulties. I hope they sell oxygen bottles there! However, I am prepared to risk the dangers in order to see the monks in their homes and try their local food. I have heard about butter tea and barley beer and hope to try them in the near future. Some of my Chinese friends would like to go too, so perhaps we will visit Tibet together."

A Problem 一个问题

Tell me about a problem that you have met in your life.
You should say: what the problem was and why it arose
how you solved the problem
if you needed anyone to help you with it
and how you feel about the problem now.

"One of my greatest problems has been in finding a girlfriend. When I was young and at school I was very shy and awkward in front of the opposite sex. I never knew how to approach them or if I did what to talk about. Perhaps because I was shy, and so had few close friends, I found it difficult to relate to other people. I was also a bit of a bookworm and preferred my own company. If there was a girl I liked then I would just admire her from a distance. I would have liked to go up to her and ask her out but I was so frightened of being rejected that I suffered alone in silence. Over the years my shyness has largely gone but I still find it difficult to get a girlfriend. Then I read an article about the numbers game. It explained that if you approached a girl and asked her out and she said no that you should then ask another girl out and so on until one finally says yes. This has revolutionised my social life and now I have no problem in finding a girlfriend."

Public Transport 公共交通

Tell me about the public transport system in your town or city.

You should say: what forms of public transport are available
whether you use the public transport system often
how it is developing
and explain how the public transport system in your town or city could be improved.

"Beijing is a fast developing city with a growing population. Like other Chinese cities there are many public buses and even a subway. Several years ago the roads were narrow and traffic was low but now things have changed. The booming economy has led to a huge increase in the number of office buildings and other developments and the number of workers and people employed in Beijing keeps rising. This has led to an increase in demand for public transport. The city has widened the roads and introduced ring roads to carry more of the increasing traffic. The subway system is to be extended. A major headache is that the demand for private cars has also vastly increased. This has led to traffic jams during peak travel times, which obviously slows down public buses. The city is trying to encourage citizens to use public transport but the SARS crisis of 2003 did not help as many commuters abandoned buses and took to taxis or bought their own car. Perhaps more bus lanes could be introduced and the extension of the subway brought forward and more areas of the city covered."

A Restaurant 一个饭店

Tell me about a restaurant that you have either been to or heard about.

You should say: what kind of restaurant it is
what special dishes are served there
where it is located
and explain why this restaurant is special.

"There are many fine restaurants in Beijing and I have not been to all of them but one I enjoyed is the home of Peking Duck. It's called Qianmen Quanjude Roast Duck Restaurant and is famous in Beijing for being the oldest Peking Duck restaurant. Many Chinese and foreigners go there, so one evening my friend and I went too. I expected a long wait, but luckily there was no queue so we were able to take our seats straight away. Of course we chose Peking Duck and enjoyed the spectacle of the chef carving our duck into thin slices right by our table. We then wrapped these slivers in little round pancakes along with spring onions and a dark spicy sauce. Duck is quite a fattening food and it does not take much for you to feel full. On the wall there is an electronic sign which flashes up the number of ducks served and eaten since the founding of the restaurant. I think this number runs into millions."

Examiners have access to these model answers.
If you copy any of them, you could get a very low score in the IELTS test.

The Role of Computers 计算机的作用

Tell me about the role computers play in your life.

You should say: how often you use computers and why
how they are important in your life
how you personally might use computers in the future
and say what new developments in computers you expect in the near future.

"Computers are very useful in my life because I use them every day. In my office I have my own computer and I use it all the time in my work. I sometimes get tired of looking at the screen all the time but it is better than writing longhand. When I am at home I mainly use computers for contacting my friends. I use email and messenger to do this and I have a wide circle of friends I chat with. I also like to play games and at the moment Solitaire is my favourite. I also like listening to music and find that there are a lot of music sites where I can download music by my favourite artists. I hate it when things go wrong with my computer because I am barely computer literate. So then I have to ask my students to help me. In future I would like to have a laptop because its main advantage is that it is small and portable and I can take it with me if I have to travel on business. I am quite happy with my computer, so I don't really want computers to develop that much now because then I would have to keep buying a new one every two years."

The Role of Money 钱的作用

Tell me about the role money plays in your life.

You should say: how important money is in your life
what you spend money on and how much you save/invest
if you spend money in the same ways as most other people
and say whether you consider money to be the most important thing in life.

"Of course money plays an important role in my life as we all cannot do without it. My major expenditure is for the rent of my flat. I suppose I spend a lot of money on eating out every month because I don't cook. I prefer to go to good restaurants as the food and service is better and I don't mind paying the extra. I have my own computer which cost about 6000 RMB, but my students helped me to choose it so it is a good one. Perhaps my mobile phone was a bit expensive but I wanted a top of the range one which would last for a long time. I suppose I spend a lot of money on taxis but they are far quicker than buses. To be honest I tend to spend all my salary, but I am able to earn extra money by taking private teaching classes. I know I should save some of my salary every month and perhaps one day I will. Money is not the most important thing in life but we all need a certain amount in order to have a comfortable lifestyle."

Examiners have access to these model answers.
If you copy any of them, you could get a very low score in the IELTS test.

The Role of TV 电视的作用

Tell me about the role TV plays in your life or your family life.

You should say: how much TV the people in your family watch
whether you enjoy the same types of programmes
how its role in your family has changed over time
and compare its role to other forms of leisure activity.

"Television is not important in my life right now because I rarely watch it. Although there are a lot of channels I find most of the shows boring. I don't like the game shows, Beijing Opera or any kind of soap opera. I do sometimes like to watch the news if something dramatic or interesting has happened but I mainly catch up on the news through the Internet. When I was at school I used to watch TV all the time, sometimes missing dinner to watch my favourite programme. And when I started work I would relax in the evening by sitting on the sofa in front of the television. Nowadays I tend to use the TV as a means of watching DVD's. I have nearly 200 and usually watch at least one every night. The disadvantage of this is that I rarely go out at night and am in danger of becoming a couch potato!"

A School 一所学校

Tell me about a school that you have attended at any time in your life.

You should say: what you learnt at the school and who taught you
what the school campus was like
whether the school and teachers were as you expected
and explain how the school helped improve your future prospects (or did not!).

"Peking University, commonly called Beida, is the most famous liberal arts university in China. In 2001, after I got my Bachelor's degree from Beijing Normal University, I succeeded in getting into Peking University as a Master's student, majoring in Regional Economics, supervised by Professor Yang, the leading Chinese scholar in this area. That's where my dream starts from because I've benefited from studying and working with the best professor and team in China. During my three years study here, I have been closely involved with the Business Development Planning of Haidian district as well as the city of Changsha. I have helped write a chapter of a book for my professor and done internships with the World Bank in Beijing and Washington. Beida is a small but beautiful campus with many attractive buildings and sights. Although I am very busy, in my spare time I like to go to Weiming Lake and relax by reading a book. In June this year I finished my thesis and graduated."

A School Trip 一次学校旅行

Tell me about a school trip that you went on.

You should say: where you went and when
why your teachers took you on this trip
what you did on the trip
and say why it was memorable.

"The school that I work for sometimes arranges special trips for the foreign teachers. One trip was a visit to the Ming Tombs. Early one morning we boarded a mini-bus and set off on the three-hour trip. There were about 8 of us but I was the only Brit with the rest being Americans. Arriving at the Tombs we explored the ones that were open and descended down into the depths. There was not a great deal to see and once you have seen one tomb then you have seen them all. Wandering around the car park I came across a family group of Chinese having lunch on the grass. They generously invited me to join them and I tried several different dishes although some of them I was not used to and therefore did not like. In the evening we stopped for a meal at a restaurant which was recommended by one of the locals. On the way home we stopped by the roadside to buy some fruit from one of the many fruit-sellers. It was dark by the time we got home and we were all tired and exhausted. A nice trip but a little too far away."

A Scientific Development 科学发展

Tell me about an important scientific development.

You should say: what the development is and who developed it
what the original idea behind the development was
how it has developed in recent years
and explain how it might influence society in the future.

"Nano-electronics is a hot new field at the moment. This is the science of making things extremely small. Electronics have come a long way since Thomson's discovery of the electron in 1897. The invention of the transistor in 1947 established a new electronic industry and the development of the computer led to a demand for smaller and smaller components. This opened the door wide for micro-transistors and microelectronics. But these were not small enough and so nano-electronics came into being. The smaller some components become, the bigger the problems. Traditional concepts and present technology are severely challenged. For example, photolithography techniques have come close to their limits and the reduction in wire size causes considerable enhancement of the effect of heat transmission. Scientists are now studying the laws of electron movements in order to develop the concept and fabrication technique of nano-devices."

A Shop 一家商店

Tell me about a shop you like to go to.

You should say: where the shop is and what it sells
something about the people who work there
why you like that shop in particular
and say whether other people have a similar opinion of this shop.

"Hamley's is one of the most famous toyshops in the world. It is located on Regent Street in the centre of London. The shop is now in a six-floor building and it is estimated that over five million people go there each year. The shop only sells all kinds of toys – train sets, chess sets, toy soldiers, model ships, computer games, remote control cars, and, most famous of all, teddy bears! Hamley's has supplied toys to Royal children since 1938. The best thing about Hamley's for many children (and maybe adults!) is that you can play with many of the toys in the shop before you decide whether to buy them or not. Obviously, this policy ensures that the shop is almost always full of kids playing – and parents wondering how much credit they still have on their credit cards!"

A Short Course 一门短期课程

Tell me about a short course you have taken or would like to take.

You should say: what the course is about
where you did it / could do it
what the exact content of the course was / will be
and say how it has benefited or will benefit you.

"In the summer of 1998 I had just finished my first year at university. A friend, knowing that I wanted to be a teacher, suggested that I take a TESOL course. Now I had never heard of this but I soon found out that TESOL stood for Teaching English to Speakers of Other Languages. There would be a special five-week intensive course held in my university that summer so I applied. There were a few difficulties before I even started the course. I had to find the money, pass an interview and find somewhere to live, but these obstacles were soon overcome. We started the course at 9 in the morning and there were different classes all day. About 20 students of different nationalities attended, including French and Chinese. We learned all about grammar and pronunciation and phonetics, but most important of all we learned to teach. We had to prepare lesson plans and then give these lessons to international students who were learning English. At the end of the five weeks it was a relief to know that we had all passed."

Something Dangerous 危险事物

Tell me about something you think is dangerous.

You should say: what it is and why you think it is dangerous
whether other people also think it is dangerous
whether this dangerous thing has any good points
and say if you think you are good at handling dangerous situations and things.

"I think that driving a car in Beijing is dangerous. China has the dubious honour of having the most car accidents in the world and to me most of them seem to happen in Beijing! It is quite common to travel the streets of Beijing and be caught up in a traffic jam caused by an accident. I have seen many such accidents where drivers have just driven into the car ahead. Most accidents seem to happen when cars overtake or are changing lanes. In Britain we have an overtaking lane and it is illegal to overtake on the inside but here in Beijing all lanes are regarded as being available for overtaking. Cars will overtake on the outside, inside and indeed any side! What makes this worse is that drivers rarely indicate their intentions of changing lanes. And inevitably accidents happen. This is why I won't drive in Beijing and prefer to let others do the driving. I am not the only one to think this way. I have many friends who won't drive here because of the danger that they may have an accident."

Something Exciting 令人激动的事情

Tell me about something really exciting you have done in your life.

You should say: what it was and when you did it
whether you were alone or with other people
if you would like to do it again
and say whether you think your life is really exciting.

"When I was at university, I used to play paintball with a large group of friends. Paintball is rather like playing 'war games'. You dress in military style clothes and run around shooting each other with guns that fire small balls of paint – hence the name 'Paintball'. On either Saturday or Sunday we would get up early and drive out into the countryside to the paintball site. There, those of us who had our own equipment would put it on. The others would rent theirs from the site operators. Apart from the clothes and gun, everyone had to wear goggles to protect their eyes. More experienced players usually had a mask to cover the whole of their face, as getting shot there was quite painful. Then we divided into two teams and went to our part of the combat zone. Each team had a flag, which was fixed to a tree at head height. The objective was to capture the other team's flag and bring it back to the place where your flag was located. If you were shot, you were out of the game. Each game lasted a maximum of 20 minutes, so you had to be quick to get out, find the enemy flag, grab it and return. It was very exciting and really got your heart pounding as you ran through a wood or across open ground, getting shot at and occasionally shooting back, hoping to hit someone and not get hit yourself."

Something You Own 你拥有的一样东西

Tell me about something you own which is useful or important to you.

You should say: what the thing is and how you got it
why it is useful or important to you
if it is also important or useful to others
and say how your life would be harder without this thing.

"My mobile is really important and useful for me. I carry it around with me everywhere and feel lost without it if I sometimes forget it. I never used to have one when I was in England but I find them really essential here in China. A lot of people have business cards and having your mobile number on it helps people to be able to contact you. I often do some part-time work so having a mobile means that I am contactable. I first bought one last year. I went with a student and we chose a Panasonic. Then I had to choose a number, put some money in it and then it was ready to use. This year I bought a new one. I had plenty of money so I decided to buy the best I could. Again I took a student with me and he recommended Motorola to me after checking out different models on the Internet. It probably has a lot of functions that I will never use but it is modern and it looks good."

A Sport 一种运动

Tell me about a sport that you either watch or play.

You should say: what the sport is and why you like it
if it is popular with other people in your family / city / country
where and when you play or watch it
and say how you feel when you play or watch this sport.

"Perhaps the only sport I watch on a regular basis is football. I never played it at school but I did play it at university. Football is probably the most popular sport in England and there are many teams to choose from but most fans support their local team. Coming from Leeds it is natural for me to support Leeds United and so I would look forward to watching live games on TV at the local pub. Now Leeds have some skilful young players so they are always exciting to watch. They have been among the top five in the Premiership over the last four or five years but recently they have not been doing well. In fact they have been so bad that last season they were relegated and most of their best players sold. I still watch football but prefer to watch my national team instead. However, England do not seem to be playing any better than Leeds."

A Sporting Event 一种运动项目

Tell me about a sporting event that you have seen or heard of.

You should say: what the event is and when it takes place
if it is popular with other people in your family / city / country
where can find information about it
and say how you feel when you see or hear about this sporting event.

"As I like football I have enjoyed watching Euro 2004. Naturally, being English, I have supported England and was looking forward to seeing England do well. As this tournament is held every four years it provides a great opportunity for our players to show how good they are and also prepares the team for the World Cup which is held 2 years later. England has established stars like David Beckham and Michael Owen but they were eclipsed by a rising new star, teenager Wayne Rooney. As I live in Beijing which is 7 hours ahead of European time, I had to watch the matches early in the morning. I particularly enjoyed watching England play the host nation Portugal and after extra time it finished 2-2. Then it was down to penalties. Now England have never done well in penalty shootouts and Euro 2004 was no exception. Captain David Beckham blasted the ball over the crossbar and soon England were out of the competition. From that moment on my interest in Euro 2004 waned and I never watched another match. It was the same in England. TV viewing figures slumped as fans switched to Wimbledon instead."

Sports Facilities 体育设施

Tell me about the sports facilities in your town or city.

You should say: what sports facilities there are
how much people use them
whether they are expensive to use
and explain how the sports facilities in your town or city could be improved.

"Beijing has many sports facilities mirroring its central role as China's capital. Here you are able to play golf, tennis, swim, practise archery and go bike trekking. There are many international standard sports stadiums and health and fitness clubs abound. Perhaps unique to Beijing are the exercise yards which have sprung up all over the city. These are areas alongside roads or by apartment blocks where brightly coloured exercise bars can be found. Beijingers like to exercise and about 5.5 million residents regularly exercise. There are nearly 3000 sports grounds where they can carry out their morning and evening exercises. With the coming of the Olympics in 2008, many new Olympic standard facilities will be built which will be opened to Beijing residents after the Games close."

A Strange or Unusual Place 一个奇异的地方

Tell me about a strange or unusual place you have visited or heard about.

You should say: where the place is and why it is unusual
if the people there are also unusual or special
what you can see and do there
and explain how you feel about this place.

"A strange place that I know is Iceland. This is an island in North-Western Europe that was first settled by the Vikings. Although a large island it is mainly covered with glacial ice and rock making it largely uninhabited. Yet many of the early Viking settlers preferred it to their own homeland. It is a popular place with tourists who like to visit the glaciers and especially the hot springs that gush out of the frozen earth. Out of a population numbering more than 280,000, half live in the capital Reykjavik and its neighbouring towns in the southwest. Iceland is a hot spot of volcanic and geothermal activity: 30 post-glacial volcanoes have erupted in the past two centuries, and natural hot water supplies much of the population with cheap, pollution-free heating. Rivers, too, are harnessed to provide inexpensive hydroelectric power. The Icelanders still speak the language of the Vikings, although modern Icelandic has undergone changes of pronunciation and, of course, of vocabulary! Iceland is alone in upholding another Norse tradition, i.e. the custom of using patronymics rather than surnames; an Icelander's christian name is followed by his or her father's name and the suffix-*son*. Members of a family can therefore have many different 'surnames', which sometimes causes confusion to foreigners!"

A Subject 一门课程

Tell me about a subject you enjoyed studying at secondary school.

You should say: what the subject was and why you liked it
how the teachers taught this subject
how important it has been, or will be, in your life
and say if you are good at this subject.

"I can still clearly remember the first chemistry experiment of my life—the decomposition of $KMnO_4$ for the production of O_2. The moment I put a dying lighted matchstick over the test tube, the stick instantly burst into flames—so did my interest in chemistry. Ever since, I became extremely passionate about reading chemistry books and executing chemistry experiments to quench my eternal thirst for chemical knowledge. By the end of the first semester of my first year at high school, I had already read through all the available chemistry course-books and finished all the experiments required for high-school studies. My immersion in chemistry experiments made a deep impression on my chemistry teacher, Mr. Wang, who was also in charge of the chemistry lab. He presented the lab keys to me, so that I could do my experiments any time I wanted."

Examiners have access to these model answers.
If you copy any of them, you could get a very low score in the IELTS test.

A Teacher 一名教师

Tell me about a teacher you have had.

You should say: who the teacher is/was and what subject(s) (s)he teaches or taught
what the teacher is/was like
how he/she taught
and say whether other people had a similar opinion of this teacher.

"Apart from parents probably the most influential people in our lives are teachers. I have had many teachers in my life, some memorable, some instantly forgettable, some strict, some laid back, some funny, some severe, some knowledgeable and excellent and some indifferent. One of the best teachers I remember taught at the local university and I attended his English literature class in the evenings. He was a slim man in his early thirties and he wore glasses. There were about twelve or fourteen students in his class and we examined the works of writers such as Shakespeare and Dickens but also modern writers like David Lodge. In his classes he emphasised that the best way to understand an author and his book was to read it several times. He patiently taught us and encouraged us to read the books as much as possible. I have found that he was right. In doing this I have learnt far more from a book than by a casual reading. I have continued to do this over the years and have encouraged my students to do the same."

A TV Programme 一个电视节目

Tell me about a TV programme that you watch regularly.

You should say: what the programme is and when it is shown
what kind of people watch this programme
how it is set out and who presents it
and say how you feel when you watch this programme.

"The TV programme that I watch the most is called CSI and is an American programme. CSI stands for Crime Scene Investigation who are an elite team of police forensic evidence investigation experts working their cases in Las Vegas. There are five members in the squad – Dr Gil Grissom and Catherine, Warren, Nick and Sara. Each week there is a mystery that can only be solved using the latest forensic and scientific technology and quirky leaps in logic. The medical scenes can be quite gruesome but I enjoy watching the plot unravel and try to guess who or how the crime was done. It introduces the latest techniques in forensics and shows that even though a crime cannot be stopped the criminal certainly can be. As I watch the show each week I have got to know each of the characters quite well as their personal lives are often introduced into the show."

The Way You Work 工作方式

Tell me about how you could improve the way you work or study.

You should say: what the improvement would be
if it would be easy to make
if you would need other people to help you
and explain why this would improve the way you work or study.

"Study is one area where I could improve. I can't say that I am very efficient in using my time well. I don't plan ahead or make out a timetable, so obviously this is one thing that I need to do. Sometimes I can work for long hours without taking a break whilst at other times I find it difficult to concentrate on my studies for more than a few minutes. I know that courses in study skills are available at my university and I have taken some but they do not seem to sink in. I know what I should do, but don't take the right course of action. One of my biggest problems lies in note-taking. I have to read an enormous amount of books for my course and this means that I should have some system of recording what I read. I could always ask my classmates how they have solved this problem and take my cue from them. If I can improve my study skills then my work will improve and then I will do better in my exams which is what I want."

The Weather 天气

Tell me about the weather in your city.

You should say: what the weather is usually like in the different seasons
whether people often discuss the weather in your town or city
what people think of the weather in your town or city
and say whether you think the weather in your town or city is better or worse than in other places.

"I live in Beijing which is near the east coast of China. It has four seasons in a year unlike some parts of China which only have one. In summer it is really hot and most Beijingers use umbrellas. This summer has been quite unusual in that it has rained a lot. Most people like autumn best. As autumn follows summer the weather is cooler and it makes it easier to walk the streets. In winter it gets really cold and often snows although the snowfalls are not heavy. Spring is a nice season when the weather starts to get warm after a cold winter. Everything comes back to life and flowers bloom and green leaves appear to give a colourful appearance to the streets and parks. There are just two drawbacks to spring. First it is too short and is practically over before you know it. Second there are sandstorms which threaten the capital with their clouds of dust bringing tears to the eyes and driving pedestrians off the streets."

Your Favourite Actor or Actress 你最喜欢的演员

Tell me about your favourite actor or actress.

You should say:
- who the actor or actress is and where (s)he is from
- which films (s)he has starred in
- why you like him/her in particular
- and say whether other people you know have a similar opinion about him/her.

"My favourite actor is the well-known Hong Kong and Hollywood star Jackie Chan. I first saw him in a Hong Kong movie several years ago and liked his fast action kung fu and funny slapstick comedy routines. He started to become more and more well-known and appeared in several Hollywood films. My favourite is 'Shanghai Knights' where he continues his partnership with Owen Wilson and travels to England to avenge his father's death and recover a stolen treasure. I once showed this film to my students in Tsinghua and they laughed and cheered throughout the film. In his latest movie he co-stars with British actor Steve Coogan in 'Round the World in 80 Days'. I was disappointed with this film because there was very little action and even less comedy. The film critics did not like it either and it bombed at the box-office."

Your Home 你的家

Tell me about your home.

You should say:
- when you started living there
- what rooms it has and what you use them for
- what your neighbourhood is like
- and say how long you think it will be your home for.

"I have an apartment in the Haidian district. I got one of my Chinese friends to help me find it. My requirements were that it should have two bedrooms and be near to my office. Finally I found one and a few days later I moved in. It is on the first floor of a 25-story high block of flats. There is a security door at the front entrance so I need a special passcard. It has a nice wooden floor throughout and a large living room. The owners left most of their furniture so I didn't have to buy much. I use one of the bedrooms as my study where I work on my computer. One good thing about my flat is that there is air conditioning in every room. The kitchen is a little small, but as I hardly ever cook that is not a problem. There are several blocks of flats in the area, so there are many people coming and going. Car parking seems to be a big problem as many of the residents have cars, but there is no underground parking provided so they have to park wherever they can and sometimes this leads to cars being blocked in. There are many small shops and restaurants in the area, so I look forward to enjoying my one year stay here."

Your Ideal Home 你理想的家

Tell me about your ideal home.

You should say: where it would be and how much it might cost
what rooms it would have
how it would change your lifestyle
and say whether you think you will ever have a home like this.

"My ideal home would be a penthouse flat somewhere in the city centre. I like the idea of living on the top of a building because then I would have tremendous views of Beijing. I would choose a building which has a lift, as I would not like to walk up all those stairs! The apartment should have at least two floors, as then the first floor could be given over to living space whilst the second floor would be for sleeping. It would be nice to have a large living room with a commanding view over the neighbourhood. There should be at least 2 bedrooms and a study and two bathrooms would be nice just in case I have visitors. I would furnish it with traditional Chinese furniture even though this is not popular nowadays. I think that if I had such a flat I would stay at home more and invite friends round more often. I hope that I can find such a flat for less than 5000 a month although if I had enough money I would consider buying."

Youth Culture 青年文化

Tell me about "youth culture" in your country.

You should say: what youth culture is
if it is different in different parts of the country
how it has changed since you / your parents were young
and explain your feelings about it.

"Youth culture in China just means the kind of things Chinese young people like to do and be involved in. You will find that it is more modern and up-to-date in the cities, especially Beijing and Shanghai, than in remote areas like the countryside and the west of China. In the cities, they like the latest fashions and will often go shopping in the big new malls or search out the trendiest or newest clothes shops. Lots of new shops and bars have appeared, not only in the city centre, but near the universities as students seem to have more money to spend. Western music is very popular, as are most western things such as KFC and McDonalds, which are always crowded. Obviously there is a generation gap and young people don't like to play Mah Jong or drink tea like their parents do. They prefer to play on their computers and drink coca-cola. More and more young people like to go to bars to hang out with their friends or make new ones rather than staying at home with their parents. I think that this is normal and part of growing up and establishing your own identity."

Student's Notes:

Part Three Topics

口试第三阶段
常见话题

Advertising 广告

What kinds of advertising can you find in your everyday life?

"Advertising seems to be everywhere nowadays. At home I normally see most advertising on TV but it appears in newspapers and magazines that I buy. At work pop-ups and adverts appear on my screen when I access websites and there are even ads in the lift. On my way home I am sometimes offered leaflets in the street and then there are always advertising leaflets in my mailbox."

Do you think that there is too much advertising in our lives?

"Definitely! I don't mind advertising in newspapers and magazines or on TV because I don't have to read or watch them but I hate those pop-ups on the Internet. There are too many of them and I seem to waste a lot of time in deleting them although you can get programmes that will kill them."

Do you think that certain products are better advertised in particular ways?

"A lot depends on the advertising budget that companies have and the specific market that they are trying to reach. It is not up to me to tell companies how and where they should spend their money."

Many people find advertising informative. Others claim it just creates demand for unnecessary products and services. What do you think?

"I think that both are true. Advertising informs you about new products and what they contain. Without advertising we would know less about goods and services on offer. As to the question of unnecessary products and services well this is subjective. What I may consider as unnecessary another person might consider necessary."

What controls should there be on advertising?

"There have to be some controls, especially regarding claims as to what some products can do. There have been some recent cases about ads about medical products being extremely misleading and this has even led to some deaths. Also there should be restrictions about pictures and images and language used. We know that sex sells anything but nobody would want explicit pictures or language being shown during family viewing or in children's comics."

Ages 年龄

Do younger people and older people have different attitudes to life?

"Yes of course, because we belong to different generations and have experienced different things. Older people have a lot more experience and tend to be more mature and wiser when it comes to making important decisions. Younger people, on the other hand, have not that much experience and tend to make more mistakes."

Do you think that young people should be permitted to do certain things (like marry, drive cars, vote) earlier in their lives (or later in their lives)?

"Different countries have different laws regarding these issues. Perhaps a lot depends on at what age a person becomes an adult. Certainly when a young person becomes an adult then he should be allowed to do all these things. However, there are exceptions. To control its rapidly rising population China encourages couples to marry later rather than earlier as is the custom in most Western countries."

Do you think that older people are really more traditional and conservative than younger people?

"Generally speaking, this tends to be true. I know that as I have got older I have found that my tastes, fashions and views tend to reflect my present age group rather than when I was in my twenties."

In what ways do people change as they become older?

"I think that this is inevitable and part of growing up. I would hate to act like a twenty-year old in a fifty-year old body."

Do you think that people should get married at a later age?

"I think that this is best. Marriage is for life and should be treated with the importance it deserves. We sometimes say 'Marry in haste and repent at leisure' and I think this is true. It is obviously better if you have the means to support your spouse and also some experience in relationships. However, it should be really left up to the individual to decide as everyone is not the same."

What can young people learn from older people?

"Everything! Older people tend to have gone through all that we will do so their advice is invaluable. We should certainly listen to them even if we don't follow their advice."

Animals 动物

Do you consider people in your country to be "animal lovers"?

"In Britain we are considered a nation of animal lovers and, after all, a dog is a man's best friend. Many families have a dog or a cat as a pet. We have animal rights and groups that look after both wild and domestic animals' best interests. Sometimes our pets are better looked after than our children!"

Do you agree with using animals for experiments?

"I would rather that animals were used than humans. I don't think that animals have the same rights as humans and a human's life is worth far more than an animal. If I had a fatal illness and could only be cured using a medicine that had been tested on an animal first, I would have no second thoughts about using that medicine."

If you could keep any animal in the world as a pet, which would you choose?

"I think I would love to have a dolphin. They are supposed to be very intelligent and can be trained to do all kinds of tricks. I would love to be in the pool and make friends with it and teach it something. Perhaps it could even teach me how to swim!"

Do you think that we spend too much time and money on environmental protection?

"I think there needs to be a balance here. For some people we can't spend enough and for others we spend too much. I agree that people are more important but we do have a duty to look after animals properly in whatever environment they happen to be."

Would it be better if people became vegetarians?

"I think that this choice is best left up to the individual. There are arguments for and against being a vegetarian. As long as animals are treated humanely and do not suffer unnecessarily when killed I don't object to eating meat. Perhaps we do eat too much meat and ought to replace some meat with more vegetables."

In what ways do people use animals?

"People use animals in all sorts of ways. We use horses for transport and for sport. We domesticate some animals, such as cows, so we can use them for food and clothing. We make pets out of dogs and cats or goldfish. Entertainment is a factor too as we like circuses, zoos and wildlife parks."

Books 书籍

What kind of books do people in your country like to read?

"Usually fiction is the most popular as this includes romance, thrillers, crime, science fiction, etc. Biographies and autobiographies also appear in best-selling lists but political biographies are not popular. The 'Harry Potter' series of books have become popular with all age groups, even though they were originally written for children."

Do you think that people's tastes in books change as they get older?

"I suppose they do. My tastes have certainly got wider and I read more kinds of books now. I still like to read thrillers and crime books, just as I did when I was younger. I don't like westerns now though."

Do men and women like to read the same types of books?

"Well, women certainly read more love stories than men do, but I would have thought that this is probably the biggest difference. Men, on average, don't like romantic books and much prefer thrillers, crime and westerns."

In the future, do you think that books printed on paper will disappear?

"No I don't. I think that printed books have lots of advantages over e-books. You can read them wherever you like, whether it's in the bath or on the train. You can write notes in them as well. E-books may become cheaper and more popular in the future, but I think we will still have printed books."

What do you think are the qualities of a good book?

"Obviously it should be liked by the reader. Sometimes you can find lists of 'The 100 Best Books Ever', but these lists are only matters of opinion and not everybody would agree. There are some writers who are generally considered authors of good books like Dickens and the Bronte sisters. I like books that keep me glued to the page with a good plot, believable characters and lots of action. If I like a certain author then I like to read all his or her books."

If you wrote a book, what kind of book would it be?

"If I wrote a book, it would be about life in a small village. I would make it funny, maybe even weird, by exaggerating people's characters. People wouldn't be a little clever or a bit humorous, they would be extremely cunning or absolutely hilarious."

Buildings and Structures 建筑物

Compare and contrast the residential buildings and the buildings where people work in your town or city.

"Residential buildings here used to be no more than six storeys high but now they can be twenty-six or more. Office buildings tend to be in the city centre whereas residential buildings are everywhere. These buildings tend to be distinct and separate but in my office block there are also residential apartments."

How do you think the design of buildings has changed over the last 50 years?

"50 years ago, residential buildings were rarely very tall. Actually, I can't remember a building having more than six floors. Rooms in flats have become a little bigger, but many offices are smaller than they used to be. All modern buildings have air conditioning, which was unheard of 50 years ago."

How do you think buildings of the future will differ from today's buildings?

"I hope they will be built to higher standards and be more environmentally friendly. They should use the latest building materials and use less energy to run. Perhaps solar power will feature more and they might have more soundproofing."

In what ways do you think that the buildings in which people live and work influence them?

"After 9.11 I know that many people did not want to work in tall skyscrapers because of the fear factor but people seemed to have calmed down more now. I don't think office buildings influence people that much because usually they don't have a say in its location, architecture or decor. Residential property is different because owners can stamp their personal style upon them."

If you could design your own home, what special features would you include?

"I quite like the idea of having a home shaped like a golf ball and which could revolve on its axis. It would have rooms decorated in different styles and periods."

Some structures are designed for artistic purposes rather than practical ones. What do you think of this?

"If it is artistically designed and looks good then this is a great idea. We all know about the Eiffel Tower and the Statue of Liberty and the crowds of tourists they draw."

Cities and Countryside 城市和农村

Compare and contrast life in cities and the countryside in your country.

"There are big differences. Cities tend to be crowded, more polluted and have heavy traffic. The countryside has less people, cleaner air and little traffic. In the cities there are modern shops with the latest consumer goods while it may be difficult to find some things in the countryside. There will be more jobs and higher pay in cities and transport and roads are better, too. Entertainment is more varied and up to date while in the countryside perhaps more traditional entertainment can be found."

Do you think that people in the cities and in the countryside have different personalities?

"It is sometimes felt that rural people are a little backward and less educated than their urban counterparts and certainly it is true that education is better in the city than in the country. Life is faster and more modern in the city and so people would be more active, fashionable and knowledgeable about the world than rural people."

When you are older, do you think you would prefer to live in a city or in the countryside?

"I would hope that I could make enough money in the city to be able to afford to retire to the countryside as then I could have a garden and maybe even some livestock."

In your country, are people moving to cities or from cities?

"Here in China there is a general trend for people to move to the cities because of more jobs and higher pay. This leads to overcrowding and traffic problems."

How do you think city (country) life will change in the future?

"I think there will be more pollution, traffic and overcrowding in cities in the future. I don't think these are problems that can be easily solved and will continue to get worse."

Do you think sci-fi films show a realistic view of future life on earth?

"Sci-fi films are just fiction. Nobody really knows what life will be like on earth in the future so how can you say that a sci-fi film can be realistic? It's just one person's creative idea of what the world will be like and turned into a film."

Computers 计算机

How have computers changed everyday life?

"Computers are now widely used in the home and office, in school and university, in shops and even in cars. We use them for education, work, leisure and communication so that every aspect of our lives are touched whether we are at work, rest or play."

What new developments in computers that are widely used in homes and offices do you expect to see in the near future?

"I expect to see voice operated computers with handwriting recognition software available. Computers will operate all home services such as cooking, heating, lighting, security and entertainment."

Do you think that the use of computers should be restricted and how?

"Computers should not be restricted but perhaps some of the software should be. We all know that students spend a lot of their time playing games or chatting when they should be studying so perhaps this kind of software should be removed. However, I don't think that this is feasible. I know that at Tsinghua first-year students are not allowed to have computers as this might interfere with their studies."

Do you think that people rely on computers too much?

"We obviously rely on them to do a lot of our work and calculations are certainly made easier. When a computer goes wrong or crashes, inevitably it means that work is either delayed or lost until the computer is fixed."

Many people say that computers are making children less intelligent. Do you agree?

"If children are using the computer then it means that they are not doing something else. This sounds obvious but that something else could be playing inside or outside with other children. Some experts argue that social interaction aids intelligence and therefore being alone in front of a computer and letting it do everything for you is not ultimately beneficial."

What new features would you like to see on personal computers?

"I would like computers not to have any new features but rather simplified versions of what we already have. I think that computers now are too technical and complicated and many existing features are never used."

Crime 犯罪

What do you think of capital punishment (the death penalty)?

"I am for the death penalty for murder as I think it acts as a deterrent and prevents the offender from killing again. I am aware of the arguments against capital punishment but feel that alternatives do not sufficiently punish the killer. After all, the death penalty is the only punishment that fits the crime. The alternative – life imprisonment – is rarely actually 'for life'. Often the killer is released after only a few years and may kill again."

Do you think that prison is an effective way to punish criminals?

"I don't think that prison solves anything. I think that although it removes the criminal from society it brings him into contact with other criminals and increases the possibility that he may re-offend. Too often, life in prison is too comfortable and it's not much of a hardship for criminals to endure."

What are the alternatives to putting criminals in prison?

"I think that for non-violent criminals there are several alternatives. The right one could be selected by experts after they have assessed the criminal. The important thing is to discover *why* the person committed the crime. If they stole money to buy drugs, then obviously the first thing to do is get them off the drugs. Violent criminals are clearly a danger and need to be dealt with in secure facilities such as prisons."

Do you think that increased violence on TV is related to increased crime?

"There are many factors that contribute to crime and perhaps TV is one of them. There is more violence shown and this could encourage some susceptible viewers to imitate what they see. Also more relevant today is that once TV and films used to show bad people getting their just rewards by being captured and sent to prison but now they sometimes become antiheroes and escape."

Are the police sufficiently trained and equipped to deal with crime?

"There is a constant battle between law enforcement, technology and crime. Modern criminals are becoming increasingly aware of the need to use more sophisticated methods and the police also try to stay one step ahead by using the latest technical and forensic methods. Sometimes it is better to put more police officers on the streets to deter crime rather than putting more technology into solving cases."

Culture 文化

In your opinion, what are the most important cultural aspects of your country / region?

"I think that music and film are very important today. There has been a great shift away from traditional Chinese music and movies to more modern Western ones. The number of bars and clubs have greatly increased as today's youth discover new ways to express themselves."

Do you think that people's cultural tastes change as they get older?

"I am not sure they do. I think we become aware of other cultures as we grow older and we try some of them, but basically we remain true to our own culture."

Are cultural events an important part of life in your country / region?

"I think that cultural events are still important but becoming less so as time goes by. The Spring Festival is avoided by more and more students who prefer to stay at college with their friends."

In the future, do you think that different cultures will come closer together or remain distinct?

"As the world becomes smaller and differences merge there is a need to remain distinct and separate. Culture distinguishes one set of people from another, one race from another, one country from another. We may become a global village but a village is made up of several households each different from the other."

What aspects of other cultures interest people in your country?

"We are heading towards a kind of supermarket culture where people can pick and mix the bits and pieces of culture they are interested in. In China people can listen to Japanese songs and read Japanese comics. They can wear the latest American fashion and eat Korean food."

How do you think that American culture is influencing life in your country?

"America influences China in many ways. We all wear western clothes, eat McDonalds or KFC, listen to American music and watch Hollywood movies. We like to drink coke and speak English with an American accent. Most students want to go to America to study or work and earn lots of dollars."

The Economy 经济

Which industries are important in your country?

"To be honest all of them are. There is a need for all industries to upgrade as much as possible and develop efficient working practices that would help them to become more competitive which would improve their industry and the economy as well."

Which industries do you think will become more (or less) important in the future?

"Any industry that does not adapt itself to modern technological advances will not survive. Industries that trade with foreign companies or countries are important because they bring in foreign currency and enable them to exchange technological advances. Hi-tech industries are becoming more important too."

If your country wishes to attract more foreign investment, how can it do so?

"The establishment of Special Economic Zones has seen much foreign investment. Allowing foreign banks to operate in China would mean that foreign investment would become easier to make as it could be done in their own language."

How can companies improve conditions for workers and encourage them to work harder?

"If work places have air conditioning, modern furniture and the latest computers then employees might work harder but a better way is to provide incentives that reward increased effort with increased pay. Bonuses can be introduced for more work done or for work completed within a time scale. Profit sharing is another idea."

What has been the most significant development in your country's economy during the last 10 years?

"I think that the involvement of foreign investment has meant that Western practices and technology have entered the country to the great benefit of China's economy."

If you were in charge of your country's economy, what main change(s) would you make?

"I would encourage industries to upgrade as much as possible by giving them subsidies and grants so that they could compete not only at home but abroad too. I would also encourage industries to move west to further develop these areas and help raise people's standards of living."

Examiners have access to these model answers.
If you copy any of them, you could get a very low score in the IELTS test.

Education 教育

How has the education system in your country changed over the last 20 years?

"There is more advanced technology used in the classrooms today with the use of TV's, computers and audio-visual material. Unfortunately, modern teaching methods have not kept pace with the new technology and there is a tendency to focus on memorisation and passing exams."

How do you think the education system will change in the near future?

"It is likely that Chinese education will become more Western styled in the future as academic exchanges increase and the need to be able to compete on a level footing with the West."

What changes would you introduce into the education system?

"I would make education more western and student centred. I would also cut the length of postgraduate courses and make them research based only. I would also encourage further participation with western universities and encourage foreign teachers to stay longer by increasing their salaries and benefits."

Do you think that education should be free?

"In my country primary and secondary education is free which I feel is good because everybody has the right to be educated regardless of income. There should be some payment for university education though."

What do you think are the qualities of a good teacher / school?

"A good teacher should know more about his subject than the textbook and be able to communicate his knowledge well in order to inspire his students to loftier heights. It does not matter about his dress but he certainly should have a sense of humour and be well organised."

Do you think that the government needs to focus more on educating adults?

"Education should be a lifelong process and not just restricted to the young. The government can increase its pool of educated citizens by promoting further education colleges and distance learning schools. Many of my older PhD students have come back to university because they need to know the latest technology in order to do their jobs well and have been encouraged by the government to do so."

The Environment 环境

What measures should the government and individuals in your country take to improve the environment?

"I think that there are several things that people can do as individuals. An obvious thing is to recycle whenever possible. This will enable us to use fewer resources. People can aid this process by separating their waste into categories – plastics, metals, paper, organic waste (e.g. waste food) – even before the waste is collected. People can use fewer resources such as water and electricity. They can also reduce the amount of chemicals they use, particularly for cleaning."

Can our environment ever be truly clean?

"Never! As fast as we clean up one mess we seem to make another mess somewhere else. We are naturally waste producing people and although we can achieve some preventive measures we can never have a totally clean environment. After all, we have left debris in outer space and on top of Mount Everest!"

What can we do to protect endangered animals?

"One way is to remove them from the danger and place them in specially equipped zoos and encourage them to breed so that later they can be reintroduced into the wild. Another way is to remove the danger from them by creating special reserves, passing laws to protect them and making sure that these laws are put into effect."

If we focus too much on the environment, won't our economy be less efficient?

"There is now a growing public awareness of, and indeed demand for, environmentally friendly products. Many products now have 'environmentally friendly' stickers on them so it is in the companies' long term interests to make sure that the environment is safeguarded and protected for future use by the next generation."

Do you think that older people and younger people have different views of the environment?

"I think that younger people may have a more idealistic view of how environmental problems can be solved whereas older people generally have a more realistic view. Younger people are more likely to be involved in organisations that campaign over environmental issues because idealist views often demand that some action is taken."

Family 家庭

How has family life changed in your country / region over the last 50 years?

"In 1978, the one-child policy came into force and this has led to a slow down in the rate of population growth. Disadvantages have been a tendency to spoil the only child, a bigger burden on the child in supporting his parents and increasing use of abortion when the foetus is female. Although the male child is still preferred the status and role of women generally, has increased and women have risen up the business and political ranks in increasing numbers."

Do you think that each person in a family should have a clear role?

"I think it helps the family if each parent has a clear role with regard to their position in the family. Ideally, both parents should discuss this either before they marry or shortly after."

Do you think it is better for families to live close together?

"I don't think it is a good idea for a newly-wed couple to live with either of their parents in the same home but it could be helpful if parents lived nearby. Then they could assist in the running of the home and looking after any children."

How do you think that family life will change in the future?

"I think that families will get smaller and that more children will seek to leave home earlier. Grandparents might choose to live away from the family home in special old people's homes."

What do you think are the qualities of good parents?

"The number one quality of a good parent should be taking time to spend with their children. Even if the parents argue and quarrel, most children prefer their parents to stay together rather than divorce. Love and care are important as well as the gift of encouragement."

How do (will) you treat your children differently to the way your parents treated (treat) you?

"I think I would try to spend more time with my children. Children grow up very quickly and these childhood years provide special and long cherished memories so I would want to be there. I also would be strict with my children regarding their homework and encourage them to do well."

Examiners have access to these model answers.
If you copy any of them, you could get a very low score in the IELTS test.

Famous People 著名人物

Do famous people have special responsibilities to society?

"If society makes people famous then famous people have a responsibility to be role models of their generation. They cannot expect to act one way in public and another way in private. This is just plain hypocrisy and should be exposed as such."

Some famous people are very rich. Is this fair?

"Some famous people are very poor too and is that fair also? We do not live in a fair world and there will always be the rich and poor and the famous and unknown. I know that I would rather be rich and famous rather than poor and unknown so why shouldn't others want that too?"

What kinds of people are famous (or "admired") in your country?

"Young people tend to admire musicians and singers as well as CEO's in business. Film stars are admired too. Older people may admire people who do good things for their country such as charity workers. Politicians are not as admired as they were."

Should the private lives of famous people be made public?

"People love to hear about other people and famous people's lives are different from others because they are so well known. Reporters and photographers follow them about and make lots of money because the private lives of celebrities is news and sells newspapers."

Do you think that monuments to famous people are a waste of money?

"In England we have lots of monuments to famous people and war heroes like Nelson's Column. Tourists flock to see them and so they have survived the test of time. Other monuments of famous people in other countries have not fared so well and we have all seen the pictures of huge statues crashing to the ground."

In Britain, for example, certain famous people receive honours and titles. What do you think of this?

"Every year in June there is the Queen's birthday honours list as well as the New Year's honours list where certain people are rewarded. Although there is always some grumbling about whether some of them, or even all of them, deserve titles and honours the majority of British people approve and secretly await their turn!"

Examiners have access to these model answers.
If you copy any of them, you could get a very low score in the IELTS test.

Films / Movies 电影

To what extent do you think that most films are realistic?

"Some of the most popular films at the box office today are not realistic in the slightest. We have the Lord of the Rings trilogy about dwarves and hobbits and elves and other fabled folk. Then there are the Harry Potter films about a boy who has magical powers to fight evil. Some films do portray real events but often in a fictionalised way as real life can be boring."

Do you think that people's tastes in films change as they get older?

"I think it's normal for tastes to change to a certain extent as you get older because you see more films and learn more about them. Your tastes tend to become more sophisticated as you age even though you may still like the same kinds of films you saw when you were younger."

Do men and women like to watch the same types of films?

"I don't think that women like to watch horror films as much as men and certainly they like romantic films more than men do. Perhaps men and women have the same taste in films as they do in books."

Are American films similar to films produced in your country?

"American films are not similar to Chinese films in any way but more and more Chinese directors and producers are learning from Hollywood advances in technology and incorporating these new techniques into their films. Some Chinese actors are now becoming well known in Hollywood."

What do you think are the qualities of a good film?

"It should have a good plot, believable actors and capture the imagination of the audience. Plenty of fast paced action, the use of special effects and witty dialogue are also sometimes considered as part of a good film."

What qualities does a good actor or actress need to have?

"I think a good actor or actress needs to have a strong screen presence and be able to assume the identity of the character he is portraying on screen. Some actors or actresses tend to be typecast into certain roles so the ability to play against type is a valuable asset."

Food 食物

What kinds of food do people in your country like to eat?

"In England we now have a huge variety of international cuisine to choose from. We have moved away from traditional British food, like roast beef, to include rice and pasta as alternatives to potatoes and French, Italian, Indian, Chinese, Greek, Thai and Mexican food are all readily available."

Do you think that most people in your country / region eat healthily?

"I think that Chinese food is more healthy than Western food as you rarely see overweight Chinese people. Vegetables are not cooked for as long as in the West and therefore retain more of their proteins, vitamins and other nutrients. Fruit is eaten in bigger quantities and there are more varieties found."

Do older people and younger people prefer the same kinds of food?

"At home they would eat the same food but younger people like American fast food more than the older generation do and are more likely to try other foreign food such as Italian Pizzas."

What kinds of food do you think will be more popular or less popular in the future?

"I think that China will follow the food trends in other countries. Certainly more foreign food will become available in shops and there will be more foreign restaurants. It is likely that organically grown food will increase in popularity."

Is food an important aspect of cultural life in your country / region?

"Yes it is! Most Chinese people greet each other with the phrase, "Have you eaten?" so the topic of food is never far away. Families like to have gatherings centred around the table and students and workers often celebrate by having a dinner in a restaurant."

If you were preparing a special dinner for 6-8 people, what would you need to do and what food would you prepare or order?

"Well first of all I would organise someone to cook the meal as I can't cook and I would leave the choice of food to them. Then I would have to arrange for a cleaner to come and tidy up my flat. I would look after the drinks and try to make all the guests feel welcome and make certain there were no awkward gaps in the conversation."

Friends 朋友

What are the most important qualities in friends?

"I think that being available when needed is an important quality as friends need to meet on a regular basis in order to maintain that friendship. Having the same interests and being able to get on with each other are important too. The ability to listen and give good advice also comes in very useful."

How are friendships different from / similar to other relationships, e.g. with family or colleagues?

"It is commonly said that you can choose your friends but not your family! However friends come and go but your family will remain your family forever."

Do men and women do similar kinds of things with their friends?

"I think that men are more likely to go to sporting events or go out for a drink with their male friends while women tend to go shopping or stay in the home chatting with their female friends. I think there must be a genetic shopping gene implanted in most women's brains as most men hate shopping."

Do men and women discuss different things with their friends?

"Actually, I talk about a wide variety of things with my friends, but certain topics do take up most of the time. Those topics would be work, women, food, sport, TV and current affairs. I know what my wife talks about with her friends, because I can hear her on the telephone! Men seem to prefer talking face-to-face over beer!"

Do you think that friendships between people of the same age are usually stronger than when the age difference is large?

"Many people agree that this is true. However, there are many cases where other factors are more important, such as similar interests or personalities. Sometimes friendships between people of different ages are so strong that they get married!"

How can friendships change as people get older?

"Ideally friendships should develop and deepen as we grow older but there are also further opportunities to become more distant. Families, jobs and interests can all be means of coming between friends as well as uniting them."

Examiners have access to these model answers.
If you copy any of them, you could get a very low score in the IELTS test.

Going Abroad Long-term 出国计划

Why do many people want to go abroad for an extended period of time?

"There is always the attraction of a foreign country, its language, culture, architecture, scenery, etc. which is appealing to most people. Sometimes the need for a change from a boring lifestyle is one reason. Work and study also play important parts. In England students often have a year abroad between school and university in order to broaden their horizons."

What should these people do before going abroad?

"Travel is simpler these days and information about other countries is widely available in books, TV and the Internet. It helps if you can actually meet someone from the country you are about to visit as they can give you detailed information and answer any questions you may have. If you are going to work or study then your employer or university are valuable sources of information."

What would you miss most if you went abroad for an extended period of time?

"Family would be the thing I would miss the most and perhaps I would be homesick for a while. I can always call my family though, or use the Internet to keep in touch with them and then there are always holidays when I can return home."

Which country or part of the world wouldn't you like to live in?

"I would not like to live in a cold country such as Finland because there is too much snow and the winters are long and the days are dark and short. I much prefer a warmer country to live in."

What are a few of the problems of living abroad and how can people overcome them?

"I think that the biggest problem is the language barrier and you certainly should try to start learning the language before you go and continue once you arrive."

Why do foreigners stay in your country for an extended period of time?

"Some foreigners really like the different pace of life, or the culture, but perhaps a romantic involvement is a popular reason for staying."

What kinds of problems do foreigners living in your country experience?

"Problems with bureaucracy are common as well as health related problems."

Health 健康

Who do you think should pay for health care?

"In England we have a state health system which is free but of course people ultimately pay for it through taxes. I think that everyone has the right to health care but it is becoming increasingly expensive to maintain and those who can afford it should pay more than those who can't."

Do you think that people take enough responsibility for their health?

"Well, some do and some don't. It's a personal decision and many people have a healthy or unhealthy lifestyle because that's their personal choice and who am I to legislate for others? We should take more responsibility for ourselves and our families by taking more exercise and eating a well-balanced diet, for example."

Do you think that the government should promote a national health drive?

"The government often does this whether it's to do with particular health problems like smoking or AIDS. In order to promote a national health drive then hospitals and health centres have to be improved and more sports centres provided. People are a country's strongest resource and need to be healthy. After all, the more healthy people are, the longer and harder they will work. That means more tax income for the government!"

How have health services improved in your country in recent years?

"In the cities they have improved a lot but in the countryside there is still a lot to do. I think the SARS panic helped to improve services and conditions immensely."

What more could be done to improve health care in your country?

"There are always improvements that could be done such as newer and better-equipped hospitals, more nurses and doctors and more research into diseases. I think that health care in the cities is up to an acceptable standard but in the countryside things are different. There is a reluctance for trained doctors and nurses to move there as facilities are poor and the salaries are low so the government should provide subsidies and other benefits to encourage them to relocate."

How well are health care staff (doctors and nurses) trained in your country?

"Medical training standards are rising every year but there is still a shortage of university hospitals for training new recruits."

History 历史

Do you think that a knowledge of history is important for a well-rounded education?

"We all need to know our own country's history, the position of our history with regard to others and world history in general. Someone said that if we fail to learn from history then we are condemned to repeat its mistakes."

Do you think that politicians and other influential people pay enough attention to history when planning the future?

"Maybe I am being a little cynical when I say that perhaps too many politicians are concerned about their role in history rather than learning from the past so that they can wisely influence the future."

Which historical event do you think most influenced your country's history?

"The bombing of Pearl Harbor by the Japanese in 1941 was certainly influential, because it demonstrated that the USA couldn't just isolate itself from world affairs. Even today, we can see the results of that event, as the USA tries to influence world events, not wait until events influence them directly."

Which historical events continue to influence the lives of people in your country?

"I think that the invasion and occupation by Japanese forces in 1937 have led to a negative view of that country and the sooner that Japan apologises the better."

In the future, do you think that history will become less important as science and technology become more important?

"A hundred years ago few people could imagine things like computers and space shuttles and televisions. Today these marvels are no longer marvellous as students and researchers discover new finds. History is the study of the past and what has already been discovered. Science and technology brings the future into the present but history only brings the past into the present. Students today are eager for new knowledge, not old knowledge."

If you could be an important historical figure, who would you choose to be?

"I would like to be Alexander the Great because he conquered the world and I haven't."

Hobbies and Interests 爱好和兴趣

Do you think that men and women usually have different hobbies and interests?

"Not always. I think the differences between men and women are getting less and less and women are challenging men in every area now so this includes hobbies and interests."

Do you think that people's hobbies and interests change as they get older?

"No I don't think so. Perhaps the amount of time devoted to hobbies and interests change over the years as you may have more time when you are younger and older but the age in between is when you are more occupied with family and work."

If you took up a new hobby or interest, what would you take up?

"I would love to take up parachuting. It is a dangerous but exciting sport and the thought of jumping out of an airplane and then flying through the air for several seconds would be breathtaking. It would be quite expensive so I would have to stop eating out at so many expensive restaurants!"

In the future, do you think that people will have more time to spend on their hobbies and interests?

"Well, certainly the working week is getting shorter, people are being given more holidays and so there is more leisure time. In the future, people will retire earlier and live longer and that means more time to spend on hobbies and interests."

What do you think our hobbies and interests tell other people about our personality?

"If you are introverted, quiet and shy then possibly your interests might reflect that as you may prefer to spend time doing an interest on your own, such as reading or stamp collecting. If you are extroverted and outgoing then you may be involved in interests that involve other people such as sports."

Do people often have hobbies or interests connected in some way with their work?

"I suppose that it would be ideal if you could combine your interests and work and probably some people do that. For example, if you are a train spotter then you get a job with the railway. It can work the other way round with a job dictating new interests."

Examiners have access to these model answers.
If you copy any of them, you could get a very low score in the IELTS test.

Holidays and Tourism 度假与旅游

What kind of places do people in your country / region like to go to on holiday to and what do they usually do there?

"Tourists like to see famous historic buildings whether they be castles or cathedrals or palaces. People are interested in the history of these places and any unusual stories connected with them. City breaks are also popular as they give tourists the opportunity to spend a few days in a European capital and explore it in their own time."

Do you think that where people go on holiday and what they do on holiday is related to their income?

"Yes, because the more money you have then you can travel to faraway exotic places such as Hawaii or Bali and stay in 5-star hotels. You can also stay there longer and have more frequent holidays. If your income is small then perhaps you can only travel within your country and stay in a caravan by the sea."

How are people's holidays different to 20 years ago and how are they still similar?

"They are different in that holidays now include further away destinations and hotel standards and expectations have risen. They are similar in that people still like to sunbathe by the sea or visit local tourist sites."

In the future, what kind of holidays do you think will become popular?

"I think that special interest holidays are becoming more popular as people have more time and money to spend on their existing interests or try out new ones."

What are the advantages and disadvantages of going on a "package holiday" where everything is prepared for you by a travel agency?

"The good thing about package tours is that everything is arranged for you from flights and hotels to excursions. A disadvantage to some people is that everything is too organised and that you have to travel in a group with people you do not know or may not like."

What is your idea of a perfect holiday?

"Everything depends on your travelling companion. A pretty girl wearing a bikini on Bali island in one hand and a bacardi and coke in the other would be ideal!"

Examiners have access to these model answers.
If you copy any of them, you could get a very low score in the IELTS test.

Languages 语言

What do you think is the best way to learn a foreign language?

"The best way to learn a language is to go to a country where it is spoken as this gives you maximum exposure to your new target language. This might not be always possible so a better idea would be to find a Chinese language partner whose English level is the same as yours or even a bit higher."

Do you think that the education system in your country focuses enough on foreign languages?

"In China, English is now taught from primary school upwards and continues right throughout university education. Even PhD's have to learn it!"

If you had the opportunity to learn another foreign language, which would you choose?

"I would love to learn Chinese as this is a language spoken by a quarter of the world's population and is a country I regard as my second home. Unfortunately, I am too busy teaching English to learn it!"

How are language and culture connected?

"Our cultural ideas and thoughts are expressed through language. In the English language we have classic literature by Shakespeare that reflects the culture of the age he lived in. Victorian novels, such as by Dickens, do the same as do books of every age."

In the future, do you think that English will become so important and dominant that other languages begin to die out?

"English is taught as a first or second language all over the world and is now the language used in the business, diplomatic, political and communication world. Other languages are naturally being relegated to second place and will find themselves being used less and less, so obviously some languages will gradually disappear."

Would it be a good idea for people all over the world to learn a single, artificial language, such as Esperanto?

"No, I don't think so as English already acts as a readymade communicative global language and has the advantage of being presently studied and learnt by nearly one quarter of the world. Esperanto is perceived today as a failure and rarely used."

Examiners have access to these model answers.
If you copy any of them, you could get a very low score in the IELTS test.

The Media 媒体

How do most people in your country get the news?

"In Britain, TV is the main source of news followed by national newspapers. I remember that in instances like 9.11 it was TV that first showed the news. Newspapers just later supplemented what had been seen on the screen."

Compare newspapers and TV as news sources.

"TV is faster and also sometimes shows live stories. Experts can be brought into the studio to discuss issues. Newspapers are often seen as more reliable and in them greater amounts of news can be presented in greater detail. Newspapers can be read anytime."

Do you think that the different media (newspapers, TV, radio, the Internet) are reliable sources of news?

"If there was a reliability ranking then perhaps it would be TV first, then newspapers, radio and the Internet last. People are more likely to believe what they see. The Internet is the least reliable because there is no control over what is posted on it."

What are the qualities of a good journalist or reporter?

"A good journalist or reporter should be independent, observant, inquisitive and good with words. They should also have the ability to communicate well and briefly."

How do you think most people will get the news in the future?

"Perhaps with the increasing use of the Internet, this form could be the major medium for bringing news to the people but there will always be a place for other media."

Do you believe that rich and influential people often control what the media tells people?

"I think that rich and influential people own the media but there are editors and governing bodies that would be a limiting factor in their influencing what was said or not said. There have been occasional instances of misuse but these are not the norm."

Do people in your country focus more on domestic news stories or on international news stories?

"In China, the focus is more on domestic issues but international ones are often important."

Men and Women 男人和女人

Generally, do you think that men and women have different characteristics?

"Yes I do. This is partly to do with genetics, gender and upbringing. Men and women think differently and so act differently. Boys play with soldiers and guns while girls play with dolls and prams and this early training also helps to reinforce male/female characteristics. We dress differently and behave differently in front of our own gender than we do in mixed company."

Do you think that men and women are often better suited to different jobs?

"It seems to be so as there are more female nurses and primary schoolteachers and the majority of soldiers are still men even though women are allowed into the armed forces. Women express love more easily than men and that is why they are in caring professions such as nursing and teaching."

Why are women rarely well represented in the higher levels of government and business?

"Although women represent 50% of the population they certainly don't represent 50% of government and business. There are many reasons for this such as sexism and a view that women will leave their jobs to have a baby and not return. Although female numbers are rising in high level jobs, sexist views still prevail."

Many people believe that "a woman's place is in the home". Do you agree or disagree with this idea?

"This is certainly the traditional view and there is a lot of merit in it. Women do have a natural role in bearing and bringing up children and when they turn to a career instead find that there are added pressures which many find difficult to cope with."

Do you generally find that you get on better with men or women?

"When I was younger, all my close friends were male but now I find that I get on better with girls and often discuss the same things with them that I would with a man."

Do you think that men and women want different things from life?

"Yes I do because you only have to look at what they want from a spouse. Women want a man who is intelligent, faithful, and in a good career while men want a women who is pretty, kind and thoughtful."

Money 金钱

Do most people in your country prefer to spend any extra money they have or save it?

"In England people usually spend all their income and use credit cards to finance additional spending so saving or investing money is not so important. Here in China people have traditionally saved as much money as they can, although younger people are increasingly likely to follow the Western pattern and spend all their income."

Do you think that money is the most important thing in modern society?

"I don't but many people do. We know that money can buy a house but it can't buy a home, it can buy medicines but not health, it can buy acquaintances but not friends, it can buy a bed but not sleep. Money is important but we need to remember that money is our slave and not our master."

Do you think that people of different ages spend their money on different things?

"Yes I do and there are plenty of market surveys that have been done that will back me up. Young people tend to have a high disposable income and spend it on music, entertainment, clothes, etc. Older people may not have as much income but they are more likely to have savings or investments."

If you had one million dollars, what would you do with it?

"I remember that one girl said she would give one third towards the poor people here in China, one third towards needy black children in Africa and the rest towards medical care here. I would not argue against such a distribution."

In the future, do you think that we will still use banknotes and coins?

"Credit cards are becoming more popular but it is still a cash society in China. I think that higher bank notes could be introduced and perhaps the banks will look at introducing plastic notes which are already being used in Thailand and Northern Ireland. These tend to have a longer life than paper."

Do people who have a lot of money use it wisely?

"The Sultan of Brunei is one of the richest men in the world. He has a large collection of sports cars, including several Formula 1 cars! He seldom uses them. On the other hand, he is also well-known for donating millions of dollars to his own people."

Music 音乐

What role does music play in our lives?

"Music plays a big role in most people's lives, whether intentionally or not. We can listen to music at home, on the bus, at work, in shops, in fact everywhere we go. Music is mobile and we can listen to it on our Walkman or through our cell phone. It seems that silence is not golden anymore and therefore not to be treasured."

Do you think that children should learn to play musical instruments?

"I think that children should be encouraged to learn both at home and at school. There are many kinds of musical instrument that can be chosen to suit the individual child. Playing a musical instrument well takes patience, discipline and hard work but encourages the creativity aspects of the developing child's brain."

In what ways can music affect our feelings?

"It is sometimes said that music soothes anger. If we listen to classical or sacred music then it can aid our spiritual side. Pop or light music can lift our spirits and cheer us up. Some heavy rock music can make us want to dance."

Compare modern music with more traditional music.

"We see tremendous and fast changes being made today as modern musical trends emerge and disappear very quickly. This is one of the most obvious changes as traditional music tended to have a long popularity. Another big change has been the introduction of 'rap' music which several critics argue encourages crime and gun violence."

Is "foreign" music more popular than "domestic" music in your country?

"Music has no frontiers and so spreads naturally to more and more countries as people listen to it on the Internet or MTV or the radio. People like to listen to their particular taste in music and if it is made by a foreign group that can show their growing international taste. It is usually the case that foreign music has a great influence on domestic music and this benefits music in general."

Do people of different ages prefer different kinds of music?

"We tend to like best the music we hear during our adolescent and student years and so each new generation likes the music of that generation."

People 人

How would you like other people to view you?

"Well, I would like most people to view me in a favourable light but this is not always possible. I would expect my closest friends and family to be more accurate in their assessment of me than a passing acquaintance. I hope people recognise my cheerfulness, optimism and intelligence as well as good looks!"

Do you think that people are often influenced by material things (e.g. money, cars)?

"It would be strange if we were not. We all suffer from envy, pride and greed to some degree. I would change my present job very quickly if I were offered a higher salary and a company car even if I did not like my new job very much."

Do people's characters change as they get older?

"It is often said that we reap what we sow and if we do good things then our characters should get better or vice versa as we grow older. Our reaction to circumstances is important too as these can have a helpful or harmful influence on us. If I experience some bad luck in my life then this may make me depressed and pessimistic in outlook."

Some scientists say that people are products of their environment. How far do you agree?

"This is the old nature versus nurture argument. I think that nature plays the biggest part in creating our character but nurture, or environment, has an important role to play and cannot be easily discounted."

What do you think are the most important qualities a person should have?

"I think that love is the most important quality as love embraces other qualities like mercy, kindness, forgiveness, tolerance and patience. If we are loving then other people accept us more easily and also forgive us more easily for any bad qualities."

Older people often tell their younger relatives to "lead a good life". What do you think they mean?

"I think that it means good in a moral sense. And it obviously refers to older peoples' traditional values. But what is 'good' for an older person may not mean the same thing for a younger person."

Examiners have access to these model answers.
If you copy any of them, you could get a very low score in the IELTS test.

Places of Interest 风景名胜

What kind of places of interest do people in your country often like to visit?

"British people often like to visit palaces and the homes of aristocrats (stately homes) in the countryside. People usually visit these places at weekends and on Bank Holidays during the spring and summer, when the weather is usually pleasant. The weather is important, as these stately homes usually have extensive gardens for visitors to walk in."

Do you think that a person's age affects what they consider to be "a place of interest"?

"Yes it does because older people like to go somewhere peaceful and quiet such as a park whereas younger people like noise and excitement that could be found in a pop concert for example."

What modern-day places do you think that people in the future will consider interesting?

"Well, cities will always be interesting but perhaps the modern buildings will not be so interesting unless the architecture is unique or outstandingly different. Perhaps sites like the Three Gorges Dam will become tourist spots."

Do you think that places of interest often also have some educational value?

"We can learn a lot from the places we visit if we consult guide books and local people. Much depends on your guide or teacher and the amount of time that you can spare in visiting. There is history to be learnt from the people who lived there and the events that happened. There is architecture and culture expressed through the buildings, too."

What *more* can we do to protect places of interest?

"Not only do places of interest need to be conserved but also the immediate area around them. It does not improve the view if we build a modern high-rise hotel next to a Buddhist temple, or build a four-lane highway nearby. Tourist numbers may sometimes have to be restricted in order to further preserve buildings and monuments. This is now being done at the Potola Palace in Lhasa. We could increase admission prices to help cover the cost of maintaining places of interest. This would probably also reduce the number of visitors."

Possessions 财产

What kinds of possessions are important to people in modern (Chinese) society?

"I think that houses are important as Chinese people like to provide for their family. Having a brand new apartment with modern Western furniture is a big trend now. Cars are becoming more important now too as people's disposable incomes rise."

Do you think that people's possessions reflect their personalities?

"Studies have shown that our personalities influence not only what kind of clothes we wear but also the colour! Red can mean that you are very emotional or passionate, for example. If a person is very neat and tidy that will also be reflected in what he wears."

Do men and women like to have the same kinds of possessions?

"Women like to have many handbags and shoes and so clothes and fashion accessories are important to them. Men are less interested in clothes but would be more likely to have the latest technological gadgets and, of course, have always been interested in cars."

Do certain possessions give people status in your country?

"I think this is true in most countries. In England designer clothes and accessories as well as the right car, address and job all give added status. For example, David Beckham has all these and is one of the most famous football stars in the world. If you have a big car, the latest mobile and an IBM laptop then other people will look and act more favourable towards you. Well, maybe that's the idea."

In the future, what possessions do you think that people will value most?

"As we get older, maybe the possessions we will value the most will be photos of our family and friends and gifts from loved ones. It is possible that people will value hand-crafted and traditional items rather than mass-produced items."

If you could possess any item in the world, what would you choose?

"I would love to own a Rolls Royce. This is the most luxurious and expensive car in the world and also hand-made rather than mass produced. To be able to drive down the road in one would be an unbelievable and unforgettable experience as they are supposed to be wonderful to drive."

Running a Business 开公司

If you could have your own business, what products or services would you offer?

"I would want to run my own restaurant. It would be a hot-pot restaurant as I would not need to hire a cook. I would buy the business from a franchise as they would be responsible for all the food deliveries and therefore it would make my life a lot easier."

What would be the best way to advertise your products or services?

"This depends on my budget. As I would be just starting and probably not have a lot of money, I would have to rely on leaflets a lot and use students to deliver them. My restaurant would be in a mall so handing out leaflets would be a cheap and effective way of reaching new customers."

On what basis would you choose your employees?

"I would want staff who were warm and friendly and were prepared to put the customer first. It would not matter too much if they had no previous experience as they could do on the job training. I would also expect them to have a high standard of personal hygiene."

What are the characteristics of a good boss?

"One who knows how to lead and is also prepared to delegate. Too often bosses run everything and don't allow others to develop their own leadership abilities. He should be approachable and easy to talk to so that employees can come to him at any time and discuss work and any problems they might have."

What benefits would you offer your employees?

"As a new business I could not offer as much as other well established businesses. I would introduce bonuses depending on turnover and profits. I would also offer generous holidays and overtime payments. Obviously meals would be free and I would give family and friends discounts on meals taken. I would introduce a suggestion scheme and give rewards for the best ones."

Do you think that it is important for employees to spend time together socially?

"I think that it is a good idea for employees to have, say, lunch together if they wish but social activities organised by the company outside work time should be optional as employees have their own personal lives and anyway, employees are free to invite their colleagues to a social activity whenever they want."

Science 科学

What kind of person do you think makes a good scientist?

"He or she should be original and creative and not afraid to take risks or to challenge the orthodoxy of his day like Galileo or Copernicus who believed that the earth revolved around the sun and not vice versa."

Do you think that modern scientific inventions have really improved our lives?

"I think that most of us would find it difficult to manage without our computers or mobile phones and find that these are really necessary in our everyday life. They have helped to make life and work easier. Health is an important area where computers and scientific inventions have done much to lengthen our lifespan and combat disease."

Do we really need people like historians, philosophers and sociologists in the modern scientific world?

"Science can tell us *how* something is but not *why* and so historians, philosophers and sociologists are still very useful even though they may differ in their conclusions."

What new scientific developments do you expect to see in the next ten or twenty years?

"I would like to see personal air packs developed that would enable people to transport themselves wherever they wanted. This would take traffic away from the ground into the air where there is more space to manoeuvre. I would also like to see homes being built under the sea as this would relieve the pressure on limited land resources."

What do you think of laboratory experiments on animals?

"I think that I would be too squeamish to actually want to see one but I think they are a necessary evil as I would rather a person's life was saved through laboratory experiments than lost without them. Especially, if it was someone I knew."

Medical science is constantly helping people to live longer. Do you think that is a good thing?

"It is better to live longer than face the alternative! But we seem to have a limited life, so that although medical science can help us to live longer we still face numerous health and aging problems that increase as we get older."

Examiners have access to these model answers.
If you copy any of them, you could get a very low score in the IELTS test.

Shopping 购物

Do you think that small shops can compete with large department stores and supermarket chains?

"I don't think they can if they are located right next door! Small shops benefit from serving a local area and are able to provide more personal service but are often more expensive than the supermarket and do not have as much choice and variety in what they sell."

Do young people and older people have different attitudes to shopping?

"I think that older people tend to be more thrifty and economical in making purchases and will have more brand loyalties. Younger people, on the other hand, are more likely to suffer from impulse buying and buy according to style and image rather than from practical considerations."

How is shopping today different to shopping ten or twenty years ago?

"We obviously have bigger supermarkets and malls to shop in and there seems to be a wider selection of goods and services to choose from. Online shopping has become popular and late night and 24/7 shopping is starting to catch on in some areas."

How do you think shopping will be different in the future?

"I think that catalogue shopping from your local supermarket might be an innovation. The ability to do online shopping and then have it delivered to your door or be able to pick it up from the supermarket would save a lot of time."

Do people in your country prefer buying things in several different small shops or in one or two large ones?

"There are so many people here that shops are everywhere. I think that shopping has mainly been done in small shops but that is simply because there were not many large ones. Now that supermarkets and shopping malls are here large shops will take a bigger slice of the cake."

When people are shopping, do they pay more attention to quality or price?

"This probably depends on the people and what they are buying. It also depends on their budget. Not everybody can afford to buy the best regardless of price. There is a big demand for cheaper food staples but people are prepared to pay more for quality as quality products are more economical in the long run."

Skills 技巧

Aside from those related to computing, what kind of skills do you think will be most useful for getting a good job in the future?

"I think that team skills are useful as companies are requiring employees to be able to work together as a team as the ability to get on with people is vital. English as a language skill is also useful as more companies are trading with foreign companies and need employees with a good command of English."

Do you think that children should learn practical and artistic skills at school?

"Both are useful as practical skills give children a sense of accomplishment as indeed do artistic skills. After all, if children do not learn these skills at school where are they going to learn them? Not all children are encouraged to learn practical or artistic skills at home."

Can having practical or artistic skills help develop people's characters?

"If we have no practical or artistic skills at all then I think that our characters are not fully developed."

In the future, do you think that certain practical and artistic skills may be lost?

"I think that these are being lost all the time but most of them refer to skills that are no longer needed or used. It is obviously more time consuming and expensive to make certain products or do some things in old fashioned ways than if we have modern technology in their place."

Which practical or artistic skills do you wish that you had?

"I wish I could be more computer literate and knew more about the various computer programmes so that I could make fuller use of them for my work and leisure time pursuits."

Do you think we can learn practical and artistic skills from books or do we really need teachers?

"Whilst the number of students enrolling for distance learning is increasing it will never replace actual onsite teacher training, as face to face teaching is the best method of teaching there is. Teachers can explain the information more clearly than books show and, more importantly, correct our mistakes on the spot."

Sport 运动

What kinds of sports are popular in your country now, but weren't popular 20 years ago?

"I think that sports like roller-blading and snow-boarding have become very popular in the last few years. There has also been an interest in extreme sports where man has to overcome certain natural obstacles or compete with others in different disciplines."

Do you think that young people spend too much time studying, watching TV, and playing on computers rather than getting exercise and playing sports?

"I would say yes. Many of my students say that they spend too much time playing games on the computer rather than studying or doing sports and that their work has suffered. I think that parents and teachers should be stricter with the children under their control but encouragement is better than enforcement."

How can playing sports help us in other aspects of our lives?

"Playing sports helps increase your level of energy, allows you to make new friends, helps prevent disease, and increases stamina. So it is common sense to take part in sports although it is usual to play less sports as we get older."

Which sports do you think will become more (less) popular in the future?

"In England football keeps on increasing in popularity but a lot depends on the success or otherwise of the national team. After England lost in Euro 2004 national interest in the game plummeted."

If you could be really good at a sport, which sport would you choose?

"I wish I was really good at football. I like it, but the main reason I would choose that sport rather than any other is that top football stars are known all over the world. Wherever they go, fans cheer them. I would love the attention! In addition, football stars earn a lot of money and that's an attractive reason for most people to do something! I could also play for the national team, which would be a great honour, though I hope I wouldn't make a mistake and let the team down."

Compare the kinds of sports that men and women prefer.

"There used to be a greater division between sports played by men and women but now the tendency is for equality in the games played."

Transport 交通

Compare trains and buses as forms of transport in your country.

"Trains are popular and cheap but often very overcrowded and sometimes it is difficult to get a ticket. Buses have the advantage of a better network but are slower than trains. I prefer a train to a bus for a long journey as I can book a soft sleeper and travel in some style and comfort."

Which types of transport do you think are better for short journeys and which are better for long ones?

"For short journeys I always take a taxi as it is quicker than a bus even though it is more expensive. For longer journeys I prefer to take a plane as it is faster than the train. Speed and comfort are more important for me than cost."

Is flying a common form of transport in your country?

"It is certainly very common and increasing in popularity. The airlines are joining forces and buying new aircraft so that new routes will be added and more flights available."

How do people in your country usually travel when they go on holiday?

"When holiday time comes all forms of transport are heavily used and sometimes it's a matter of having to take what's available. Buses are better for short destinations, trains and planes for longer ones. People who have cars may prefer to use those."

Do you think that the use of cars should be limited by law?

"I certainly think so. In the big cities we already have too many cars on the road and this increases pollution and traffic jams. The problem is that we have too many cars on the road now, so restricting future car ownership is not going to help all that much. Perhaps something could be done about the taxis, many of which drive about the city empty."

In what ways do modern transportation methods make our lives easier?

"We can visit more places, travel faster and in more comfort today than ever before. It can be easy to book a holiday from home using the computer and we can pay by credit card too. The downside is that in some places and at certain times there can be too much traffic and this can cause delays."

TV 电视

How much do you think that TV influences our lives?

"TV provides us with current affairs, entertainment and informative programmes. Most households would have one so the potential for influencing our lives is tremendous. We can use TV as a means of relaxation after work or study and be kept informed of what's happening in the world. However, sometimes we can be too involved in watching other people's lives rather than in living our own."

Do you think that children watch too much TV?

"Parents often think this although children don't! Watching too much TV may mean that children are not doing other things, such as homework or interacting with other children. Parents need to keep a balance between the passive and active activities their children are involved in."

Do you think that there is too much advertising on TV?

"No, I don't think so. I think the amount is just right at the moment but perhaps it will increase a lot in the future. Some advertising is not allowed, such as for tobacco products. If it was allowed we would probably have too much advertising."

Compare the kinds of programmes that young and old people watch.

"Young people watch a lot of music shows and modern soap operas whereas old people tend to like traditional dramas and game shows. Both watch news and current events but generally there is a big difference between the programmes they watch."

Is there too much violence on TV in your country?

"We are used to seeing a lot of kung fu on Chinese TV, so you could say that violence is a way of life! However, the violence shown is not as graphic as shown on Western TV, so I would say that there is not too much violence shown."

Are many foreign TV programmes shown in your country?

"Not many. Certainly not within domestic TV networks, although this may change in the future. The ones that are shown tend to be very old programmes or films. There are foreign TV channels available but they are expensive to subscribe to."

Work 工作

What kinds of jobs do you think will be the most popular in the future?

"There are usually trends within the job market so that what is popular now may not be popular in the future. One career that is popular now and will remain so in the future is anything connected to an international company. These jobs are seen as offering higher salaries, prestige, the opportunity to mix with foreigners and the possibility of travel abroad."

Do you think that salary is related to the importance of the job?

"I hope so. As I progress up the corporate ladder I would expect to receive a higher salary. This is true in most areas. I know that nurses are not highly paid and yet they are considered to have important jobs."

What other factors can influence the salary a person earns?

"A person's relevant education and experience are big factors in deciding the initial salary. Increasing responsibilities and length of service usually lead to promotion and a salary increase. Having additional skills such as a language and passing language exams are important factors too."

What factors influence young people when they are deciding on their future jobs and careers?

"Job security is highly important as is a job related to their major. Salary is important too, but because of the intense competition for jobs this is now not as important as it used to be."

If you had your own business, what would it be and what kind of people would you employ?

"I would like to run an English school and hire native English speakers who are qualified teachers and good at communicating with students. I would have classes connected with IELTS and business so I would need experts qualified in these fields."

In the future, do you think that people in your country (or occupation) will work fewer hours or more?

"The trend worldwide seems to be for fewer working hours and China is no different from other countries in this respect. There may well be government regulations that will come into force restricting the number of hours that employees will work."